# KEEP

Practical advice for t

*Also in this series*
BEFORE AND AFTER BABY COMES
CIDER APPLE VINEGAR
COMMON COLD
CONSTIPATION, HAEMORRHOIDS AND COLITIS
EATING FOR HEALTH
HEART AILMENTS
HIGH BLOOD PRESSURE
HONEY, NATURAL FOOD AND HEALER
IMPROVE YOUR SIGHT WITHOUT GLASSES
KEY TO FITNESS
LIVE LONGER AND HEALTHIER
LIVER AILMENTS AND COMMON DISORDERS
LOSE WEIGHT AND GAIN HEALTH
MASSAGE AT YOUR FINGERTIPS
NERVE TROUBLES
RAW JUICES FOR HEALTH
RHEUMATISM AND ARTHRITIS
SKIN TROUBLES
STOMACH ULCERS AND ACIDITY
VITAMINS EXPLAINED SIMPLY
WOMAN'S CHANGE OF LIFE

# KEEP YOUNG AFTER 40!

*Prepared and produced by the Editorial Committee of Science of Life Books*

Revised and extended by
Vivienne Lewis

**SCIENCE OF LIFE BOOKS**
11 Munro Street, Port Melbourne, Victoria 3207

Second Edition, revised,
enlarged and reset, 1985

© SCIENCE OF LIFE BOOKS 1985

*Registered at the G.P.O. Sydney
for transmission through the post
as a book*

*This book is sold subject to the condition that it shall not, by way of
trade or otherwise, be lent, re-sold, hired out, or otherwise circulated
without the publisher's prior consent in any form of binding or cover
other than that in which it is published and without a similar
condition including this condition being imposed on the subsequent
purchaser.*

Inquiries should be made to the publishers:
Lothian Publishing Company Pty. Ltd.
11 Munro Street, Port Melbourne, 3207

U.K. Distributors:
**THORSONS PUBLISHING GROUP**
Wellingborough, Northamptonshire

U.S.A. Distributors:
**THORSONS PUBLISHERS INC.**
New York

National Library of Australia card number
and ISBN 0-909911-13-4

Printed in Great Britain by
Richard Clay (The Chaucer Press) Ltd,
Bungay, Suffolk

# Contents

| | Page |
|---|---|
| *Introduction* | 7 |

*Chapter*

| | | |
|---|---|---|
| 1. | Research into Long Life | 13 |
| 2. | A Well-balanced Diet | 22 |
| 3. | The 'Wonder Foods' — Including Raw Juices | 50 |
| 4. | Exercise | 70 |
| 5. | Health and Beauty | 87 |
| 6. | Giving Up Alcohol and Smoking | 112 |
| 7. | Take a Look at Your Life | 119 |
| | *Index* | 127 |

# Introduction

We have lived through the Youth Cult for over a quarter of a century. But now in the mid-eighties we are seeing a new phenomenon; middle-aged people who look like youngsters, jogging around in track suits, exercising in leotards. With the benefit of better nutrition, dance and exercise classes springing up everywhere, many interests to keep the mind active and colourful fashions worn by people of all ages, people are looking younger than ever. They've got the examples of film stars like Jane Fonda and Joan Collins to follow — middle-aged women who still look terrific.

But there are still too many people who hold on to the old-fashioned idea that once the age of 40 is reached, it's a downhill slide to the grave, with middle-aged flab, false teeth and a feeling that the best part of life is over. They could not be more wrong. People can enjoy the best years of their lives between 40 and 60, and beyond that too. In their middle years they can prepare themselves for an active healthy elderly life — up to their century!

Most people are not seriously ill, but nor are they healthy.

Many health experts believe that more people could live active lives right up to their advanced years if they did not poison their bodies with over-refined starchy foods, white bread, white flour products, white sugar, biscuits and cakes, but instead switched to a good routine of regular wholefood eating. Our rich Western food, laden with sugar and fat, has made us the poorer in terms of health, with heart disease, diabetes, cancer and so many bowel disorders resulting from our lifestyle and our diet. The body does not wear out. Instead it becomes infected or poisoned, starved of vitamins and minerals. The system simply breaks down under the strain.

Races have been discovered in various parts of the world who live to great ages — in the Hunza region of Pakistan, for instance, in the Andes in South America and the Caucasus region of southern USSR. Longevity is the norm, not a rarity, in these regions. Well-attested ages of a century and far beyond have been recorded. Many reasons have been put forward to account for this phenomenon — from living on a diet of mainly yogurt and honey, to vegetarian eating, lack of stress, and the minerals present in the soil, particularly the trace element selenium. A combination of some or all of these ingredients makes up the recipe for a healthy long life.

Industrialized nations tend to regard 70 as old, when in fact many more people could reach 100 if they followed a few simple rules. The rules are easy — the harder thing is to carry them out consistently, and that requires some willpower. But if the end-product is a happier longer life, then that is in itself an incentive to make the effort.

It does mean the rethinking of some values. It does mean realizing that your present way of life is not necessarily the best for your health. Look at yourself critically. Do you have vibrant health? Do you have an abundance of energy? Probably you have lots of niggling little ailments, aches and pains here and there. In time these small irritations could lead to a major illness. But by altering your lifestyle a little, by taking more exercise and changing your diet, you could say goodbye to illness.

Premature old age is a sad thing. There is no need for it to happen to anyone. Yet we ignore the signs of the onset of poor health — persistent constipation, piles, blotchy skin, nervous irritability, colds and coughs.

One of the ways in which it is thought that people age more quickly is through a build-up of acid in the body over a period of years. As Dr George W. Crile, one of the pioneers in this field, said, 'There is no natural death — all deaths from so-called natural causes are merely the end point of a progressive acid saturation.' This acid saturation is progressive almost from the moment of birth, according to Dr William Howard Hay, writing in his book *Health Via Food*. He outlined the four sources of acid accumulation, four ways in which people kill themselves. He put it very simply: 'Such death is always unnatural, because it has violated Nature's provision for health, and is a suicide just as is the knife or pistol.'

Dr Hay saw the first source of acid formation in people eating too much protein — often ten times as much as the body needs for tissue replacement. Although protein is the body-building material, it is also the most acid-forming. For an adult, around 45g a day is thought to be sufficient, but most people eat far more than this. Babies, children and teenagers need the most protein as they grow, but as their rate of growth slows down after puberty, their need for such vast amounts of protein also decreases.

The second source of acid is found in the foods all too often seen on shop shelves — processed, refined foods, white flour and white bread, white sugar and all the foods made from them, all robbed of their normal alkalis and therefore acid forming.

The third source of acid build-up is harder to understand but the idea is strongly held by such proven nutritionists as Doris Grant, famous for her bread recipe. This is the use of foods, whether good or bad in themselves, in mixtures that are not compatible. So, to eat meat and bread at the same meal, or meat and then a heavy starchy pudding, results in a fermentation which produces a lot of acid in the body.

The last way in which the acid build-up in the body gradually occurs is linked with the other three factors. This is the scourge of the Western world — constipation. Food stays in the colon for too long without being moved on and out of the body, and in the meantime it ferments and putrefies. That is why a constipated person is never well, usually lethargic, often depressed and in time will probably endure a major illness.

Constipation is a rarity in the Third World, where only natural unrefined foods are eaten. In the Western world constipation causes colitis, diverticular disease, varicose veins, appendicitis, and leads to heart disease and cancer of the colon. If only white bread was cut out of the diet and wholemeal eaten instead the change would be remarkable in time. With the increased fibre in the diet by taking more wholegrains such as wholemeal flour, constipation would decrease, especially if other refined foods were replaced by a whole new shopping list consisting of whole grains such as brown rice and oats, and more fresh vegetables and fruit. If you stick to a diet with these foods, plus more beans and pulses, constipation will become a thing of the past, even as you get older, and an energetic healthy life will replace it. Above all, cut down on the amount of food you eat, as being overweight makes you look older. Fashionable, smart, young-looking clothes don't fit. You have to seek comfort and so you eat more — it's a vicious circle, affecting men and women alike. Your outlook on life ceases to be youthful and energetic, you become an old person before your time — and are in danger of dying before your time. Too many people eat mainly snacks and skip meals altogether. People who live alone, and the elderly, are especially at risk, undernourished because their basic food is often poor, and they rely on quick, easy-to-prepare snacks to save cooking, fuel and food bills. But natural foods needn't be expensive and they can be easily made — a few root vegetables in a stock makes an excellent stew or soup, padded out with bran or barley. Wholemeal bread, grated raw carrot and cottage cheese make an excellent lunch. The very minimal result of not eating properly is lethargy, headaches, insomnia, and nervous troubles — the end result is illness.

Many people realize nowadays that by eating a lot of hard animal fat, such as lard, butter, and hard margarine — and most of us in Britain still do — we lay up trouble for ourselves. Deposits of fat, called cholesterol, collect in the blood-stream, the arteries leading to the heart become clogged up, harden, and cause heart disease. Many more people know these facts but not enough has been done about it. In America heart disease has been on the decline for several years because of health education. In Britain we still have a long way to go, and have among the highest rates of heart disease in the world, but at last people are being advised by doctors to cut down on fat and other harmful foods. It is possible to slow down the rate of decline into heart disease — even in middle age. In many cases the deterioration of hardened arteries can be reversed. This book outlines the ways in which everyone, not just the lucky few, can stay healthy and young-looking after the age of 40 — and way, way beyond.

# 1

# Research Into Long Life

Many explorers and research scientists have been amazed to discover, in remote regions around the world, people who live to incredible ages. To become a centenarian in these places is a very ordinary occurrence. These people don't merely claim to be 120 or 130. Local records prove that they are right. These races — in the Hunza region of Pakistan, the Caucasus in the USSR, and in the Andes mountain range of South America — lead active, useful, healthy lives long after they have reached their century.

Dr Sir Robert McCarrison was physician to the Viceroy of India in the days of the Empire, and was also a pioneer dietitian. He saw the Hunza people and admired their health and physique. He was able to compare them with the people who lived — or rather existed — in the southern region of India. There, around Madras, he saw the effects of malnutrition due to a diet based on polished refined rice, robbed of all nutrients. The Madras people received few vitamins, minerals or body-building proteins from their diet. Hardly any milk, fruit or vegetables were eaten. They drank coffee with sugar and they chewed the betel nut. As a result sickness and early death were all around the doctor as he travelled about. There were no old grandparents to be seen. It was rare for anyone to live beyond 40. The average life expectancy was 24.

In dramatic contrast, the Hunzas were lean and fit, strong and long-lived. They were great fruit eaters, and their diet consisted of simple natural foodstuffs. They ate little meat and drank goat's milk. Dr McCarrison wrote:

> The power of endurance of these people is extraordinary: to see a man of this race throw off his scanty garments, revealing a figure which would delight the eye of a Rodin, and plunge into a glacier-fed river in the middle of a winter, with as much unconcern as many of us would take a tepid bath, is to realize that perfection of physique and great physical endurance are attainable in the simplest of foods, provided these be of the right kind.
>
> These people are long-lived and vigorous in old age. Among them the ailments too common in our own people — such as gastro-intestinal disorders, colitis, gastric and duodenal ulcer and cancer — are extraordinarily uncommon, and I have no doubt whatever in my own mind that their freedom from these scourges of modern civilization is due to three things:
> (1) Their use of simple, natural foodstuffs of the right kind;
> (2) their vigorous outdoor life, and (3) their fine bracing climate.

The doctor concluded, 'With the Hunzas, resistance to infection is remarkable . . . Cancer is so rare that in nine years' practice I have never come across a single case of it.'

Dr Howard Hay, writing of Dr McCarrison's work said:

> He found natives who were so old that it would be hard to believe their records correct, yet he was not able to detect

possible errors in their way of keeping these records.

Ages up to and well beyond a century were very common among them. He found men of well attested age up to 100 years and over recently married and raising families of healthy children.

Men said to be well over one hundred years of age were working in the fields with younger men and doing as much work as any, in fact, looking so like the younger men that he was not able to distinguish the older from the younger.

Beyond a small amount of milk or cheese, which were considered luxuries, the rest of the food consisted of grains eaten in their normal state, nuts, vegetables, and fruits and most of this was eaten raw.

He reported that these people were never sick; they had none of the diseases of the civilized countries. They could not afford to cause them.

Dr Hay went on to say that in Dr McCarrison's nine year post with the British Army Medical Service, which brought him into contact with the Hunzas, no major or even minor illness was ever discovered among the people. 'Is it possible that these people live so long and are so free from disease because they live very largely on the natural foods? . . .' asked Dr Hay in his book, *Health Via Food*. 'The largest mass evidence of longevity is that furnished by Sir Robert McCarrison and surely comprises enough instances to make a sort of criterion that favours natural foods.'

## The Research of Sir Robert McCarrison

It is worth taking a look at the research carried out by Dr McCarrison because of its historical interest in terms of nutrition. The doctor qualified at Queen's University, Belfast, in 1900. When he sailed for India to join the Indian Medical Service he was just 23. He was posted as regimental medical officer to a region on the Indian frontier and he soon showed his aptitude for, and love of, research. In 1913 he was transferred to the Central Institute in Kasauli which was well equipped with laboratories, staff and literature. In 1927 he was appointed Director of Nutrition Research in India under the research Fund Association. He was the only officer engaged to work on nutrition.

For his work he chose albino rats. His small community of rats lived in conditions modelled on those of the Hunza people he had seen and admired. They had plenty of air, sunlight and clean living conditions. The diet given the rats was the Hunza one — flat bread chapattis made with wholemeal flour, sprouted pulses, fresh raw carrots and fresh raw cabbage. They had unboiled milk, a small meat ration with bones once a week and plenty of water, for drinking and washing.

Dr McCarrison observed 1,189 rats from birth to 27 months (when rats reach the equivalent age to 55 in man). Then they were killed and careful post-mortems were carried out. They were found to be free of disease. 'During the past two years there has been no case of illness in this "universe" of albino rats, no death from natural causes in the adult stock and, but for a few accidental deaths no infantile mortality', Dr McCarrison told the College of Surgeons in a lecture in 1931. 'Both clinically and at post-morten examination this stock has been shown to be remarkably free from disease. It may be that some of them have cryptic disease of one kind or another, but if so, I have failed to find either clinical or microscopical evidence of it.'

The doctor went further. He fed other sets of albino rats on diets of the other regions of India such as Bengal and Madras, diets with poorer quality nutrition. He fed over 2,000 rats on diets consisting of rice, pulses, vegetables, spices and perhaps a little milk. These rats were not as fortunate as the first set of rats. Soon they were hit by a variety of ailments and diseases. It was a salutary lesson for the researchers to see these rats, fed on the typical diet of millions of people, contract disease of every organ, from the eyes to the bladder. They were generally weak and irritable; they showed a loss of hair, bad teeth, ulcers, crooked spines, distorted vertebrae and so on.

In another experiment Dr McCarrison gave a set of rats the diet lived on by the poorer classes of Britain at the time — white bread, margarine, sweet tea, boiled vegetables, tinned meats and cheap jams. On this diet not only did the rats grow badly but they showed signs of nervous irritability. They bit their attendants, and after two weeks of the experiment they began to attack and eat the weaker ones in the colony. Female rats given these poor diets had problems in conceiving or with pregnancies, which were often brief. They contracted inflammations of the womb and ovaries and these led to abortion or premature birth. Often they simply died in pregnancy.

## Research in Russia

One of the world's foremost experts on longevity is a Russian, Dr Alexander Bogomolets. He has said (on his own sixtieth birthday) 'It may sound paradoxical but a man of 60 or 70 is still young. He has lived only half his natural life. This is not difficult to prove.' He has also written: 'One can and must struggle against old age . . . It can be treated just as any other illness because what we are accustomed to regard as normal old age is actually an abnormal, premature phenomenon.'

Bogomolets has spent most of his career studying longevity. The Bogomolets Institute in Kiev sent a special expedition to Abkhazia in the Caucasus mountains. There they found a dozen people whose ages ranged between 107 and 135. All of them were extraordinarily healthy. One of them, a junior member of the group at 107, told the researchers that he was planning to get married! Bogomolets and his colleagues insist that these cases are not freaks. Elderly people such as those found in the Caucasus mountains can be normally expected in a healthy society where human beings live naturally healthy lives. For example, the Institute recorded the statistic of 30,000 centenarians (many of them well beyond that) in the USSR in the early 1970s.

## Honey and Long Life

In another piece of research in the USSR, a list of 200 centenarians were invited to give details of their lifestyle. The replies, which came back from 150 of them, revealed one connecting thread. A large number of them were bee keepers. All of them said their principal food had always been honey. Throughout history, writers and scientists have told of the wonder qualities of honey. Pliny in AD 76 wrote about the bee-keeping region between the Appenines and the River Po in Ancient Rome in his tax records and showed that there were 124 people living their who had passed their century. Nearer to our own times, Dr William Arbuthnot Lane strongly recommended this delicious food as a heart and muscle stimulant and as a source of energy. He maintained that there was no better food to combat muscle fatigue and exhaustion.

Honey contains about 40 per cent of levulose or fruit sugar, and 34 per cent dextrose or glucose. It also contains vitamins and minerals. Unlike other sugars it does not irritate the digestive membranes nor, like white sugar, does it neutralize the calcium in the body which is so necessary for strong teeth and bones and for the nerves, lungs and heart. Honey is a marvellous source of energy, far superior to white sugar which gives a quick 'peak' of energy and just as quickly drains away. Honey has a natural and gentle laxative effect and is rapidly and easily assimilated. It spares the kidneys and reduces tissue destruction.

Some nutritionists and members of the medical profession are apt to refute the use of honey in the same way as they do other sugars, for, if taken to excess, it will do harm, just like any food. But it is a natural food containing many nutrients, and while people want to sweeten their food surely this is the best way of doing it, along with naturally sweet fruit. It has been said that a food which has been stored for a hundred years, (as honey has in some cases) without losing any of its food value, certainly must have rather special qualities!

## Other Research on Longevity

Another seat of research in the USSR, called the Institute of Gerontology, is looking at the lifestyles of such men as Shirali Luslimov, whose claim to fame was that he was the oldest man in the Caucasus region until his death in 1973. One of his brothers had died at the age of 134 and another brother of 106 also lived in the same village, in the mountainous area of Azerbaijan where the USSR faces across to Iran. This region has attracted researchers of many nationalities, looking for the secrets of longevity. A study on one village in the region with a population of 1,200 showed that there were 71 men and 110 women between the ages of 81 and 90. Nineteen were over 90. The people of this region were once nomads. They eat hardly any meat. They rely on fresh fruit and vegetables such as beans, onions and many root vegetables. They eat great amounts of garlic. They never eat sugar. In the study of the elderly people in this village hardly any signs of heart disease were discovered. There were no cases of cancer reported in a nine year period of study of 123 people who were reputed to be over 100 years old.

An Englishman, Dr David Davies, has spent much time studying the people living in a beautiful valley in Ecuador, deep in South America. He travelled to the Vilchamba Valley in the Andes, where he found many centenarians and other old people living and working on the land. Dr Davies, from the Gerontological Unit of University College, London, was able to check the ages of the villagers, and found that there were baptismal certificates for people of 120 and 130 years of age. He was also shown death certificates of villagers who had died, in the 1920s and 1930s, at the incredible age of 150.

Dr Davies linked their longevity with the facts that the area had a total absence of heart disease and cancer, probably due to the diet of the people which was simple in the extreme — green vegetables, cabbages, marrows, pumpkins, fruit, maize, soya beans, cottage cheese and eggs. Hardly any meat was eaten. The people were also experts on herbs which were used as medicine as well as for cooking. In the nearby towns and villages, away from the mountains, where the diet was based on refined foods, such as polished rice, white sugar, tinned foods and white flour, the diseases associated with Western civilization were common.

One interesting fact emerged in Dr Davies' study of the Andean centenarians. Although the killer diseases of adult people were not to be found, infant mortality was high. About 40 per cent of children died before they reached their fourth year, catching viruses and epidemics and having no resistance against them. The survivors however, grew up with immunity to many diseases and after adolescence were robust and hardy.

So the village was not developing because it was away from so-called civilization and was protected from diseases geographically. Contact with towns and villages further away meant that viruses and infections could be brought in but the people grew up to be resistant to disease because of their healthy lifestyle.

The link between these people who live in such remote areas of the world is the simple life they lead. They work the land and grow their own vegetables. People don't retire and sit waiting for death to come. They work all their lives, producing their food and are always needed by the community. How different from so many people in the Western world, who retire in their sixties and expect to 'take life easy'. Many of them die early in retirement, from disease and often lack of motivation to carry on, or they spend years in a nursing home or hospital. Old people in Britain and the USA, for example, are rarely as active as the peasants of the Andes, the Caucasus or the Hunza regions. There are many more old people in our community than there were years ago, but their lifestyle often makes them want to die younger rather than endure years of inactivity, boredom and loneliness, with friends and companions long gone, and families thinking of them as just a burden. In the peasant communities however, the very old people are respected and looked to for advice. Their active lifestyle, right up until their death at such a ripe old age, is based on simple living and a natural diet. That at least we could try to emulate.

# 2

# A Well-Balanced Diet

You cannot be healthy through your middle years and enjoy a happy, active later phase of your life unless you eat wisely. That doesn't mean just making sure that you eat three square meals a day, although regular eating habits become even more essential as you get older, or conditions such as hypoglycaemia (low blood sugar) can be a problem. Your diet must be well-balanced, with enough proteins (though not too much — most of us in the Western world lay up trouble for ourselves in later years by taking more protein that we need) and carbohydrates and fats of the right sort. Here again, most people eat too much of these foods as well. In fact we tend to eat too much of the wrong foods in each category and not enough of the right sort.

Cut down on fat and sugar of all kinds. Eat less meat, more wholegrains, more wholemeal bread and brown rice, varying it with soya flour and rye or barley grains. Cut out hard animal fats that lay down fatty deposits of cholesterol in the arteries, and switch to polyunsaturated vegetable fats. Stop using white sugar, along with all other refined foods such as white flour and white bread — use fruit or honey as your natural sweeteners. Eat fresh salads and fresh fruit and vegetables, preferably raw, each day. In this way, with the wholegrains you eat you will be getting enough fibre for your needs. These are guidelines only — what each individual needs varies with their sex, size, and lifestyle. Some people put on weight more easily than others and have to watch the amounts they eat. Others may feel a little under par and may need to adjust their diet, although they can't pinpoint any trouble in themselves.

When we are very young we can often get away with a poor diet — it is only as we get older that faulty eating habits over the years will show themselves up as major illnesses. We cannot see our arteries to check if they are clogged up with cholesterol. Unless we have our blood-pressure taken we don't even know very often if we have high blood-pressure (there are no usual symptoms; some people may have headaches and feel anxious but this is not always the case).

Despite advances in medicine and knowledge of nutrition, life expectancy is not all that good. Serious infectious illnesses no longer trouble young people, but in middle age heart disease and cancer hit our society very hard. Although other factors such as smoking, alcohol, stress and heredity play their part, few experts doubt now that diet plays a major role in many of the diseases still prevalent today in the Western world. We don't have to look very far to find the causes. Over the past century or so, food has become more and more refined — all the techniques of flour milling have reduced flour to a fine powder, taking out all the nutritious bran and wheatgerm. We have become too dependent on white bread, white flour, and white sugar, bought in the supermarkets along with foods that are a far cry from their natural state — foods that are over-processed due to modern technology in factories, with many additives such as chemical colourings, flavour enhancers and preservatives. While not all of these additives are known to be harmful, we are beginning to realize that they are not doing us any good and some may be causing allergies and illnesses.

One of the scourges of our society is obesity — something that only affected the rich in days gone by. Again we can see the reasons all around us. We eat too much, of everything. We all take less exercise, we walk less, we ride in cars and other transport much more than people did years ago, and many of us have sedentary jobs that involve little or no muscular effort. As we are less active, so we burn up less energy. But we eat probably more than many people could afford to do years ago, and foods are richer as well. So the excess is laid down as fat on the body. We have cut down on bulky foods like bread and potatoes, which give us fibre and make other foods pass quickly and easily through the body. Instead we eat fattier, more sugary foods. If you say that you don't eat a great deal — think of the snacks and drinks, the sweets and alcohol you perhaps consume throughout the week. It all adds up! It amounts to heart disease and cancer for many people over 30, let alone 40. It adds up to other illnesses — gallstones, diabetes and strokes, and on an everyday level, headaches and migraine, indigestion and constipation.

## Fats

This is the group to think about as you get older. Fats are a very concentrated source of energy. It is easy to eat too much of them if you do not lead an active life and then you will become overweight. The fats that build up inside the blood vessels, mainly cholesterol, are a major factor in causing heart disease. The body produces some of its own cholesterol, and gets the rest from meat, eggs and dairy produce. If there is too much cholesterol in the blood the excess is deposited in the inner walls of the blood vessels where it can eventually lead to a hardening of the arteries. If nothing is done to stop this accumulation then a heart attack may occur.

Most of the fats we eat are made up of fatty acids — and there are many different kinds, with three varying basic chemical structures. Saturated fatty acids contain all the hydrogen they can hold and they are stable. Then there are the monosaturated fatty acids which can take a little more hydrogen, and thirdly, polyunsaturated fatty acids, which can take a lot more. Linoleic acid falls into this category, oleic acid into the middle group and butyric acid is a saturated fatty acid.

Studies have shown that saturated fatty acids make a high amount of cholesterol in the blood-stream, while it is also thought that the polyunsaturated types probably help to reduce cholesterol. The middle group appears to be neutral. Saturated fatty acids are mostly found in meat, egg and dairy products such as cow's milk and hard cheeses. Polyunsaturated fats tend to be from plant sources. One way of finding out if a fat for spreading on bread is polyunsaturated is to take it out of a very cold fridge or freezer and see if it will spread easily. Hard animal fats — butter and some margarines — will stay in lumps and will not spread but the polyunsaturated types will spread fairly easily. They are usually made from sunflower, safflower or some other vegetable oil. Some plant fats, however, such as coconut oil and palm oil, are highly saturated. Some naturally unsaturated fats may be artificially saturated by forcing in extra hydrogen during food processing. So the only way to know that you are actually getting polyunsaturated products is by carefully reading the labels on margarine packs: if it doesn't state that the product is polyunsaturated then it will not be. Remember that all fats, whether they are saturated or polyunsaturated, are equally calorie laden. All fats should be limited. Reduce the use of fats in baking, and at the table. Try not to add fat to vegetables but add herbs instead. Grill foods rather than fry them. Roasts are fat-laden, especially as the fat content of meat these days is very high.

It is interesting to recall the fact that people in Africa and Asia rarely suffer from heart disease and that it is generally thought to be because their diet is low in fat and calories. But when some of them move to parts of the Western world and start to follow our eating patterns and lifestyle, then they start to contract heart disease as well.

Follow the examples of other cultures — try cooking the stir-fry way in the Chinese tradition. Vegetables are lightly cooked for a few minutes in very little fat, so they retain their nutritional value. Cut down on meat and step up consumption of fresh vegetables and fruit. Experiment with new recipes, especially vegetarian ones from other countries.

If you are cooking with meat, cook the dish the day before. After it has cooled down, skim off the fat that will rest as a layer on the surface of the casserole or pot. Dry roast your meat, don't baste it constantly, and seal the juices by turning up the oven high for the first ten minutes during cooking. Use a non-stick frying pan and use polyunsaturated corn oil instead of lard. Buy lean cuts of meat and try to mince your own beef to make sure that it is not extremely fatty. Trim your meat well before cooking. If you prefer meat to vegetarian meals, have chicken or other non-fatty poultry quite often, and eat more fish (but not fried in batter or breadcrumbs).

Eat more salads and instead of putting meat into sandwiches, include more cottage cheese and vegetable fillings. Eat potatoes in their jackets rather than fry them. Limit your weekly consumption of eggs, and poach or boil them rather than fry or scramble them in fat. Eat more natural yogurt and fresh fruit for pudding rather than heavy pastry pies and fatty cakes. Ice cream contains a lot of hard animal fats as well as many additives — yogurt again is far, far better for you, your waistline, your teeth and your blood. Try drinking herb teas rather than tea with full fat milk, or switch to goat's milk or skimmed milk instead. There are many low-fat cheeses available so cultivate a taste for them — there is no need to give up every pleasure! Camembert is much lower in fat than Brie, and Ricotta has even fewer calories. Cheddar, Stilton and cream cheeses are very high in calories.

## Carbohydrates

We all know that flour and potatoes, biscuits and cakes are all carbohydrates. So why are we urged to eat more wholemeal flour and potatoes when all diets used to cut them out? There is a difference between natural carbohydrates from whole grains and potatoes and the type of over-processed, refined carbohydrates, often laced with salt and sugar, that we see on our supermarket shelves. Pure carbohydrates are not fattening in themselves and if we are on a diet we should cut down on those energy-rich fats first.

Weight for weight, potatoes have about a quarter of the calories of a steak and only a tenth as many calories as a similar weight of butter. In fact it is usually the case that people fatten themselves up with potatoes fried in hard animal fats, or mashed with creamy milk and butter or hard margarine. A jacket potato baked in the oven, and filled with a cottage cheese or similar low-fat filling will provide a good source of carbohydrate, fibre and very little fat. A slice of wholemeal bread is not in itself fattening — it is the fat that we spread on the top which piles on the weight. We would do better to cut thick wedges of bread again as people used to do, and scrape a thin layer of fat over the top.

The sort of carbohydrates we should avoid are the white flour, white sugar-based ones. The type we should eat are the whole grain cereals, brown rice, barley, oats, rye and wholemeal flour, foods that were once part of our staple diet and which remain so for many healthy people around the world. Try experimenting in your baking with the various flours — soya flour, rye flour, rice flour, and sample the different tasty results. Eat wholemeal pasta instead of the pallid variety usually bought, and you will notice how much more nutty the flavour is.

As well as the starch carbohydrates there are the sugar carbohydrates. There are various types of sugar, some of it is glucose and some is fructose (fruit sugar) but all of it should be kept to a minimum. We don't need sugar to exist but a sweet tooth is indulged among children and they become accustomed to the taste. We know now that too much sugar causes tooth decay and leads to obesity which in turn will lead to illness. Even raw brown sugar, honey or molasses (the vitamin-rich treacly substance left behind by sugar production) can cause these disturbing results if taken to excess. Eat just a little of the natural type if you like but severely limit it.

Remember that you are consuming sugar when you eat fruits and that it is more concentrated in dried fruits such as sultanas, raisins, figs and dates. Most starch foods change into sugar while going through our digestive system — especially potatoes, carrots and of course fruit again, like pineapple and grapes. Even the malic acid in an apple is turned into sugar during the digestive process. About five per cent of milk is sugar, known as milk sugar or lactose.

All these sugars are natural, valuable sugars — and they are vastly superior in nutritional value to refined sugar, so always try to use them instead of the packet kind.

## Protein

Protein is the body-builder of food. Our skin, muscles, lungs and internal organs consist of protein. Every cell, every drop of blood in our body is built of protein. Every day the body burns up about four ounces of protein tissue, even if we are engaged in the lightest physical work. This must be replaced to maintain our normal weight. Proteins are compounds of carbon, hydrogen, oxygen and nitrogen, made up of various structures of about 20 amino acids which are in a long list of combinations. The body can manufacture some of the amino acids it needs but the rest have to be obtained from food.

We need protein most when we are young and growing fast, but after puberty, although the need slows down somewhat, we still need protein for continual replacement of body tissue. The body cannot store amino acids, so if protein is eaten in excess the surplus is converted into glucose in the liver and either stored as body fat or burnt up as energy. It is not true that working people, especially men, need masses and masses of protein. Youngsters need it the most — the peak at puberty for boys is between 50 and 75 grams a day; for girls of the same age between 44 and 58 grams a day. An adult intake of around 45 grams a day is considered to be sufficient, though some people exist happily and healthily on less and others can take vast amounts of protein without becoming ill as a result. We do tend to eat too much protein in the Western world, however, and of the wrong sort.

Proteins have always been divided into two types, animal and vegetable. Animal proteins consist of meat, dairy produce and fish. Vegetable proteins consist of potatoes, beans and pulses, grains such as rice, barley, oats and rye, and nuts. Animal proteins were once called the first class proteins, the vegetable type the second class ones. Consequently, it was thought that vegetable proteins were inferior and not so essential for health. So now we eat far too much of the animal type, which also happen to be laden with fat. It is also expensive, and in today's shortages we are finding out more about this. Far more land and energy are needed to produce meat and dairy produce than for the production of vegetable proteins such as cereals or beans. Some crops are grown just to feed animals which in turn feed us — when this could be short-circuited by growing the crop for human consumption in the first place rather than to fatten up animals for the table.

Some vegetable proteins are practically as high in value as meat, especially the soya bean, which is now made into meat substitute (called tvp, or texturized vegetable protein). There are a whole range of beans and pulses to vary the diet, and the humble potato is an excellent source of vegetable protein. So nowadays we tend not to think of vegetable proteins as second class.

Apart from the high fat content in meat and dairy produce, they are high in calories and if you are not to become overweight as you get older, you will have to cut down on them. Try to eat as much vegetable protein as possible — wholemeal bread, potatoes, brown rice and other cereals, beans and pulses. Keep mainly to the low-fat sources of animal protein such as white fish and low-fat dairy produce.

### Fibre
Although fibre is the fashionable word in nutrition, it is not a new idea. Doctors have been telling people to get enough

roughage for decades, even centuries, and way back in history more or less the same was said, although in less scientific terms. Doctors and others in the field of nutrition have come to realize over the past fifty years or so that many of our ills in the Western world are caused by the lack of fibre in our diet, which has been so refined by modern food producing techniques that for example, the goodness of wheatgerm and bran is milled out of white flour, and rice is cleaned and polished to a gleaming white leaving out the goodness of the wholegrain. Most people eat foods that are over-refined and over-processed, with the natural goodness crazily taken out and wasted. Good examples are white bread, white flour, cakes, pastries and biscuits and breakfast cereals that are little more nutritious than the cardboard box they are packed in! We even peel and scrape the valuable fibrous skins off our potatoes and other vegetables! As a result our fibre deficient diet has been responsible for the increase in constipation (for many British people a way of life) and the illnesses that prolonged constipation can lead to — bowel disorders, diverticular disease, varicose veins, appendicitis and cancer of the colon.

It is thought that we should be eating around 30 grams of fibre each day. Most people in the Western world eat only 20 grams a day on average. In Africa or Asia, countries where the incidence of bowel illness is rare, the people live on a diet high in fibre and low in fat and sugar, and on average, they eat more than 60 grams of fibre daily. The study of the rural Africans and Asians made by doctors like Denis Birkett concluded that it was their diet that made them so healthy and free of constipation, colitis and all other bowel complaints. It was only about thirty years ago in this country that people were given sloppy, baby-type food when they had bowel disorders, so as not to 'disturb' the bowels and aggravate the condition. The treatment is very different today with our increased knowledge about the complaint.

Fibre works in this way. It increases the bulk of the stool in the intestines, speeding up the transit time of waste through the body. It soaks up other foods and carries it along, diluting toxins produced as food passes through the system. Constipated people don't have a bowel movement for two, three or even several days. The bowels should be opened every day easily for if food stays long in the intestines then bacteria breeds and over a period of time habitual constipation causes illness. The very minimal effect of constipation is to feel bloated and lethargic. You feel heavy and indeed if you do not take enough fibre in your diet you will become overweight, with the added risk of contracting heart disease, diabetes or cancer.

In our affluent society we have turned our backs on bread and potatoes, the staple diet of our forefathers, and now eat more meat and dairy produce instead. People are now realizing that they must include more fibre in their diet — and thankfully wholemeal bread and jacket potatoes are becoming popular once more. British people have still a long way to go before their diet is fibre-filled and healthy. Just sprinkling bran on a breakfast cereal that is in itself refined and processed is not enough because bran only contains one type of fibre. Fruit and vegetables are valuable sources and they also contain vitamins and minerals. So try to eat a wholefood breakfast, with a muesli, bought or home-made from oats, nuts, fruit (either fresh or dried or both) and sprinkled with wheatgerm. Eat wholemeal toast and enjoy the nuttier flavour and texture. Make your own wholemeal muffins, scones and flapjacks. It's not only healthier, but also tastier than the bland flood made from over-refined ingredients.

Eat brown rice and other wholegrains — there are many to choose from in health food stores. Try wholemeal pasta instead of the white variety, and include beans and pulses in your main meals. Leave the skins on potatoes, unless they are green, and don't consign the outer leaves of vegetables and saladstuffs to the bin. They are a valuable source of fibre, so shred or chop them and add to casseroles and soups. When you are baking, using wholemeal flour or, if you find it too heavy, part wholemeal flour which is also available. Usually labelled as 85 per cent wholemeal flour, it has some of the bran already sieved out. Alternatively you could sieve the bran out and add it to soups and savoury dishes.

A point to consider: if you are not used to a great amount of fibre in your diet then a dramatic increase may cause flatulence, which is very uncomfortable. Increase the fibre in your diet steadily over a period of time — say a couple of months. In this way your system will be able to adjust to the change gradually.

## Vitamins

There is no need to suppose that as you get older you need to take vast amounts of vitamin supplements to keep youthful and full of vitality. You should be getting enough vitamins from your food in the first place. You may find that there are special times, during or after illness or in times of stress for instance, that your vitamin needs are greater and then you may need to take extra care. There are 13 known vitamins — and more is being discovered about them all the time. The biggest group is the B complex, which has a variety of numbers and names.

Fat-soluble vitamins, such as vitamins A and D, can be stored for long periods in the body. The water-soluble vitamins — vitamins C and B — cannot be stored in the body and need to be replaced daily in the diet. There is an outside chance of taking too much A and D in supplements as it is stored in the body for a time, but most people are deficient; there should be no risk if you maintain a balanced diet and follow packet instructions, if taking supplements.

*Vitamin A* is essential for a healthy skin, good eyesight and resistance to infection. The best sources are fish-liver oil and liver, eggs and dairy produce. Carotene (which converts to vitamin A in the body) is found in carrots, spinach and other dark green or yellow vegetables. Deficiencies cause night-blindness, so make sure you get vitamin A if you are a motorist. Membranes of the eyes and lungs may be more prone to infection with a lack of this vitamin. It is stored in the liver, and so a deficiency is only likely to become apparent over a period of time. Vitamin A is thought to protect against many types of cancer, but it is certainly not proven that vitamin therapy is successful in cancer patients. As already mentioned, an excess of vitamin A can be toxic. Too much carotene can turn the skin yellow — so don't drink great quantities of carrot juice. A balanced, moderate diet should not pose any problems, though.

*Vitamin B complex* consists of at least a dozen vitamins. *Vitamin $B_1$* (thiamin) plays an important part in giving energy, preventing fatigue, keeping the nerves sound and promoting growth, appetite and reproduction. If you have enough of this vitamin you will have good digestion and easier bowel movements. It is found in many foods, including potatoes and milk, but especially in nuts, beans, brewer's yeast, wheatgerm and peas. The major disease connected with deficiency of vitamin $B_1$ is beri-beri, rarely found in this part of the world.

*Vitamin $B_2$* (riboflavin) helps to keep our skin healthy and our sight good. It also helps to burn the body fuel to produce energy. A sign of deficiency may be sores around the mouth. It is found in liver, milk, eggs, green vegetables and yeast extract.

*Vitamin $B_6$* (pyrodoxine) has been used very successfully in treating premenstrual syndrome and other menstrual disorders. Depression is one symptom of deficiency. It is of great value in keeping the nerves relaxed and preventing the muscles getting too tired, thus it is used in neuro-muscular disorders. It is essential in the formulation of haemoglobin in the blood. Some women may find themselves deficient if they are taking a contraceptive pill containing oestrogen. Vitamin $B_6$ is found in liver, wholegrain cereals, peanuts and bananas.

*Vitamin $B_{12}$* guards against anaemia, and osteo-arthritis. It is needed by cells in the bone marrow and the gastro-intestinal tract. As it is found in animal and dairy produce and not in vegetables (unless it is fermented with micro-organisms which is in itself unhealthy) there is a risk that strict vegetarians may be deficient in this vitamin. If no meat or dairy produce is eaten at all, then vitamin $B_{12}$ supplements should be taken. As it is stored in the liver for up to two years then a deficiency may take a time to appear if a person switches to a vegetarian or vegan diet.

*Nicotinic acid* (niacin and nicotinamide) is found in small amounts in many foods but up to a quarter is lost in cooking. It is needed for the utilization of food energy. The body can produce its own nicotinic acid but make sure you get enough supplies of meat, fish, wholegrain cereal, pulses, peanuts and yeast extract. Skin troubles such as pellagra, where the skin becomes dark and scaly, especially in the light, can be signs of deficiency.

*Folic acid* is found in all living matter, but the best sources are bread, eggs, rice, pulses, bananas, liver, leafy vegetables and oranges. It has the same function as $B_{12}$. A deficiency may cause anaemia. It can be toxic for epileptics — some drugs used to treat epileptics, likewise some oral contraceptives, can stop the absorption of folic acid. Make sure that you get enough fresh fruit and vegetables each day, raw if possible, as cooking destroys a lot of the vitamin. Folic acid is also supposed to help keep the natural colour of the hair in the middle years.

*Pantothenic acid* is necessary for growth and the steady working of the metabolism. It helps to prevent premature ageing of the skin, greying of the hair, baldness and other signs of advancing years. It helps all stressful conditions and also allergies, which are usually stress-related. You can obtain it from many foods, but yeast, egg yolk, pulses, royal jelly and the offal of meat such as kidneys are all good sources.

*Biotin* is valuable in giving vital energy and in keeping your weight normal. Again found in offal, also in egg yolk, dairy produce, cereals, fish, fruit and vegetables, so a deficiency is most unlikely.

*PABA* (para-aminobenzoic acid) is important in promoting the normal functions of the glands, especially important as you get older, as is its role in preventing hair from going grey. It is found in wheatgerm and brewer's yeast principally but also in a variety of other foods.

*Vitamin C* (also called ascorbic acid) has had entire books written about it, so great is the interest in this particular vitamin. It certainly does seem to be an important vitamin in stopping premature ageing. Basically we need it for healthy tissues throughout the body, especially the ones that connect, like cartilage in bone; it also helps the absorption of iron in the body. Research has shown that it is valuable in building up resistance to infections — probably why it is a good defence against the cold although not a cure for it. It gives strength and elasticity to the walls of the blood vessels, the gelatine basis of the bones, the ligaments and scar tissue. Wounds, ulcers, broken bones and other injuries will heal up much more quickly and effectively if vitamin C is taken.

The first sign of vitamin C deficiency is to see your gums bleeding and it can result in the faulty formation of dentine in the teeth and in the bone. Get a good supply of the vitamin from citrus fruits, green leafy vegetables, blackcurrants, green peppers, new potatoes (old ones have less of the vitamin because of long storage and probable exposure to light) and liver. It will stop premature ageing symptoms from appearing and you will feel more vital. High doses can, over a long period, cause the formation of kidney stones, and nausea, but as vitamin C is not stored in the body high doses can be safely taken to fight off a cold or flu for a few days.

*Vitamin D* is known as the sunshine vitamin — and that is probably why we need to make sure we get a good supply in other ways in this country! In warmer sunnier climates, half an hour's sun on the skin is reckoned to be sufficient for the body to provide enough vitamin D. However, this diminishes in winter, with the sun's weaker rays, and with our changeable climate we need to get the vitamin from other sources such as fish-liver oils, in liquid or capsule form. Oily fish, herrings, mackerel, pilchards, sardines, and salmon are the best food sources. Vitamin D can be obtained from eggs but as they are high in cholesterol it would be better to get this particular vitamin from a varied diet. We need it for the absorption of calcium, which makes the bones strong, and for activating the calcium in the blood-stream. Without vitamin D calcium will not work properly in the body, and bones, nerves, teeth and tissue will be damaged as a result. A deficiency, which causes rickets in children, has the effect of softening the bones in adults, a condition called osteomalacia. On the other hand, too much of the vitamin can lead to the excess being deposited in the kidneys, causing damage. One good serving of oily fish each week should provide enough vitamin D. If you manage to get your vitamin D from summer sun, remember that the ultraviolet rays (which trigger the skin to produce vitamin D) will not penetrate dark clothing or through a glass window.

*Vitamin E* Wheatgerm is the best source of vitamin E. You can also obtain it from eggs, wholemeal bread and wholewheat cereals, sunflower oil and broccoli. There is no actual conclusive proof of the effects of vitamin E, and research is continuing. It is believed to be good for the heart, helping to dilate the millions of minute blood capillaries in the body, improving blood circulation, strengthening and repairing muscle, nerve and scar tissue. It is unlikely that on a well-balanced wholefood diet any adult would be deficient in vitamin E, although it is given in high doses to heart patients in vitamin therapy. As far as is known, we cannot take too much vitamin E.

*Vitamin K* is essential for blood clotting and is found in leafy green vegetables such as spinach, cabbage and lettuce, and in cereals. It can also be made by bacteria in the intestines. It is not available as a supplement and no deficiency is likely to occur.

There are several points to consider when cooking, so that you don't destroy valuable vitamins and minerals. Firstly, don't soak vegetables for a long time before cooking, however convenient it may be to prepare them well in advance because their food value will deteriorate. Chop up vegetables immediately before cooking, for the same reason. The finer vegetables are chopped the more rapidly they lose vitamins as a larger surface area is exposed to oxygen. Avoid copper pots and pans, for they can cause oxidation and loss of vitamin C. Use saucepans with close fitting lids to restrict the amount of oxygen which gets to the vegetables during cooking.

You can cut down cooking time by using a pressure cooker. Potatoes cooked in this way can keep up to 80 per cent of their vitamin C. With any sort of saucepan, keep the cooking time down to a minimum, and use very little water. Bring it to the boil before adding the vegetables to reduce the time they spend in water and to drive off dissolved oxygen.

Never add bicarbonate of soda as it kills both the B and C vitamins. As boiling will inevitably lead to vitamin loss in the water, try steaming vegetables instead. Never pour the boiling water down the sink after straining vegetables — it is full of minerals and vitamins and should be kept for adding to soups and main course dishes needing vegetable stock. Always eat your vegetables straight after cooking — if you keep them hot you will be losing more vitamins in the process.

## Minerals

Recently, more prominence has been given to the importance of minerals in the diet, after years of interest in newly discovered vitamins. Now we are realizing how vital are minerals, even traces of them, for our health. Many people know something about calcium — we need it for our teeth and bones, we know — and iron — that's necessary for the blood. But what about the others? Magnesium, potassium, manganese, zinc, iodine, fluorine, selenium, and the rest? Research carried out in the past twenty years or so has revealed that a lack of minerals in the diet may cause people to contract the most common diseases of later life. What has emerged recently is the importance to health of the minor or trace elements in the diet. They are required in tiny amounts but the lack of them can prove just as serious as a deficiency of the minerals needed in greater amounts.

A mineral is mined from the earth and is a compound substance consisting of two or more atoms. For example, common salt is sodium chloride, which is the metal sodium combined with the non-metal chlorine. Minerals in their natural form consist of a metal and a non-metal part. In most cases the nutritional value lies in the metal part and the rest is not needed by the body. There are though, certain elements, such as sulphur, phosphorus and iodine, which are not metals but are still most essential to the normal working of the body, and the body makes use of them as well.

Some minerals are present in highly concentrated forms and the daily intake of these must exceed 100 mg of each. These include calcium, magnesium, sodium and potassium. In most well-balanced diets people will be getting enough of these minerals. The other groups of minerals and trace elements are just as vital to health but they are needed in progressively smaller amounts. The important thing to remember is that all the minerals should be present in the body as a balanced whole, each complementing the others. Some do not work unless they are in combination with another mineral.

Deficiencies arise when the soil in which food is grown is lacking in a particular mineral, or when minerals are lost during food processing, refining and cooking. There are wide areas of the world where the land is zinc-deficient and the animals feeding there have had to be given zinc-enriched feeds. Similarly, there are many places where iodine is absent from the soil, resulting in the prevalence of goitre (swollen neck tissue caused by a lack of iodine). Research has shown that in certain areas of France, the lack of magnesium in the soil has been responsible for a high incidence of cancer. Other evidence of cancer has been found in countries like Poland, caused by a lack of minerals in the soil.

Food processing, refining and cooking also causes loss of minerals. Wheatgerm is the richest source of trace elements in the whole of the grain of wheat. When it is removed during flour refining the loss of minerals and trace elements is staggering. Three quarters of the iron, potassium and sodium present is lost in refining; nearly as much of the copper, phosphorus and calcium, and most of the cobalt, manganese, chromium and magnesium. Although iron and calcium are replaced, to a certain extent, none of the trace elements are put back and there is no certainty that the replacements are used by the body in the same way as in the original whole grain. Raw sugar is also high in minerals but all the minerals are lost in refining. All that is left is pure sucrose, empty calories without any goodness. When food is cooked, the minerals tend to be released into the cooking water, and unless this water is used as a stock afterwards the minerals are completely wasted.

*Calcium.* Milk, cheese, wholemeal bread, flour and green vegetables are the best sources of calcium. Apart from needing the mineral for our healthy teeth and bones (working together with vitamin D) the body also needs it to keep the nerves and muscles steady and relaxed. People with calcium deficiency are irritable and nervous, highly-strung and tense. They are also often subject to cramps, which shows a deficiency. Illnesses caused by deficiency are the same as for vitamin D — particularly bone-softening (osteomalacia) in adults. Calcium keeps the blood clotting normally, the muscles in good repair and generally looks after the cell structure of the body bone and tissue. Calcium will also give deep sound sleep, so it is with good reason that people take a warm bedtime milky drink. Daily needs will be met by drinking between half and one pint of milk and eating three ounces of cheese.

For calcium to be efficient in its work, it must have enough phosphorus — one without the other is of little value. Phosphorus is a part of each of the billions of cells in the human body. It is a constituent of all glandular secretions and body fluids. Animals will die more rapidly from a lack of this mineral than from any other. Fortunately it is found in most foods we eat and there is little danger of becoming deficient in it. Both minerals need vitamin D alongside them to be active. Ideally no more than twice as much phosphorus as calcium should be taken. An adult needs two grams of phosphorus a day — and this should be obtained in a normal wholefood diet.

*Iron* is one of the minerals we know quite a lot about, as it was one of the earliest to be discovered. While many of us are aware that we need it for strong healthy blood, few of us realize that we need more of it in our daily diet. Numerous studies have shown that anaemia is a common ailment in our society. Women, particularly during their menstrual cycle, are vulnerable to anaemia. It may be fairly slight, but it can build up with each month's loss of blood. Tiredness, listlessness, a general lack of vitality and a pallid skin are the common signs of anaemia, which is caused when the body fails to produce enough red corpuscles, or the haemoglobin is below normal amount and so is too pale. Sometimes both conditions happen at once — there may be too few red corpuscles and too little haemoglobin. In this case not enough oxygen can be carried to the cells throughout the body, and the carbon dioxide poisons cannot be completely removed. In a cubic millimetre of blood there are normally over five million red blood cells, or corpuscles, and the number of red corpuscles is called the blood count. It varies with each person depending on their health, but when a person has a low blood count they are suffering from anaemia. A regular supply of iron in the diet will help to prevent this condition. The richest sources are liver, molasses, wheatgerm, egg yolk, spinach, dates, apricots, lettuce (outer leaves especially), parsley, soya beans and their by-products, dried fruits and prunes.

*Iodine* is another mineral about which we have known for quite a long time. A trace of it is vital to health — a deficiency causes goitre, an enlargement of the thyroid gland of the throat. This is an attempt by the body to overcome the lack of iodine by developing a larger amount of tissue to produce thyroxin. In the case of toxin or exophthalmic goitre, too much thyroxin is produced and the body starts to race. The heart beats too rapidly and a pulse of between 130 and 180 is often recorded in such cases.

In most places there is enough iodine in the soil to ensure that the very small daily requirements are obtained from the food grown on it, but in certain places where there is a deficiency in the soil, goitre is very prevalent. These are sometimes known as 'goitre belts' and there is an area in Derbyshire where there have been so many cases of goitre that the condition has become known as 'Derbyshire neck'. People living in these areas of known iodine deficiency are advised to take kelp tablets to make up for the lack of the mineral. Other sources are seaweed and seafood. Signs of deficiency include a slowing down of the metabolism and circulation.

*Potassium* is found in most foods, especially milk, potatoes, fruit or vegetable juices, yeast extract, dried prunes, Brussels sprouts — even coffee and milk chocolate. It is necessary for normal growth and repair in the body, regular bowel functioning, steady nerves and for the muscles to work efficiently. Where there is a deficiency, constipation is usual and the mind becomes over-active, resulting in restlessness and sleeplessness. The heart beats slowly and irregularly and the heart muscles become damaged. In extreme cases it can result in heart failure. Potassium works together with sodium in the body, making all cells healthier. This balance is important, especially for maintaining water balance. Potassium may also offset the effects of too much sodium in the body, which is a common occurrence in the Western diet. An excess of potassium is excreted through the kidneys so there is no fear of a build-up. A mild deficiency may occur if a person frequently takes purgatives or diuretics for water retention.

*Magnesium* is an essential part of the make-up of all the body cells and it exists in our bones. We also need it for the functioning of some enzymes. A deficiency is rare, though, unless there has been a high mineral and vitamin loss through an attack of diarrhoea. Magnesium is found in many foods, especially vegetables, although the body only absorbs about half of the magnesium received in the diet.

*Zinc* works in the body by helping wounds to heal and in the activity of about twenty enzymes. It is found in many foods, especially meat, whole grains, pulses and beans and seafoods, notably oysters. Too little zinc causes stunted growth. Studies in Iran and Egypt showed that dwarfism, which is prevalent in certain areas, was caused by a low intake of zinc. There was no lack of zinc in the diet but what was present was rendered useless by the type of unleavened bread eaten in those parts. The bread was prepared from high-extraction wheat flour which is high in phytic acid and fibre, both of which stop zinc from being absorbed in the body. Other factors such as low intake of animal foods also contributed to the problem.

Wound healing after an accident or a surgical operation is slowed down by zinc deficiency. Patients recovering from burns tend to lose zinc by excretion and if the metal is not put back in the diet healing is very slow. But once recovery of normal blood levels has taken place, zinc supplements do not have any further effect.

A lack of zinc stops the release of vitamin A from the liver, where it is stored. This means that there will be low levels of vitamin A in the blood, and so some signs of deficiency in this particular vitamin may have a shortage of zinc as their root cause. Low amounts of zinc have been found among people suffering from lung infection, liver disease, tuberculosis, kidney disease, diabetes, rheumatiod arthritis and a long list of other illnesses. Alcoholics have also been found to be deficient in zinc. This does not mean that zinc shortage is the cause of these illnesses, but that supplements are needed to keep up the zinc levels and to stop other deficiencies becoming apparent.

Women on the contraceptive pill sometimes suffer from skin troubles which may be caused by a lack of zinc caused by the synthetic hormones in the Pill. Many drugs in fact cause zinc to be excreted from the body, especially the corticosteroids, and when patients stop steroid therapy it has been found that their loss of zinc slows down. Low-protein, high-starch diets also cause a loss of zinc to the body. Pregnant women also tend to be deficient in zinc, so a supplement should be taken. Other signs of zinc deficiency are loss of appetite, mental lethargy, the loss of the sense of smell, and hair problems, including baldness. They could occasionally be the first signs of more serious illnesses but are more usually reversed with zinc supplements.

## Sodium — do we get too much?

Sodium chloride — salt to most of us — is the most common mineral found in foods. It gives two essential elements to the body — sodium and chloride (which is not the same as chlorine, a highly dangerous poisonous gas).

Sodium is present in all the fluids in the body. We need it to maintain our water balance and for muscle and nerve activity. It is important that it is complemented by enough potassium in the body.

As salt is found in so many foods, and as we add more in food processing, in cooking and at the table, there is no danger of a deficiency. Quite the reverse, in fact. We eat too much salt for our own good and in the last few years research has shown that too high a salt intake is linked with high blood-pressure, which can in turn lead to heart attacks. Only in extremely hot countries, when people sweat a lot and lose salt along with water in perspiring, is there a need to take extra salt. Athletes, people suffering from sunburn, or those who have been doing hard manual work in a warm atmosphere, may temporarily be short of salt but for most of us an excess is the problem. Under ordinary conditions an intake of about three of four grams a day is enough, but many people take far greater amounts of salt in their diet — even as much as 20 grams a day!

Foods from animal sources — meat, fish poultry and dairy produce — contain more sodium than do plant sources. Seafood tends to be higher in sodium than fresh water fish. The vegetables that contain more sodium than others are beetroot, carrots, celery, kale and spinach. Salt is hidden in many processed foods such as bacon, cold meats, sausages, smoked fish and canned vegetables. It is also in butter, margarine, cheese, bread, some breakfast cereals and in yeast extract. It is present in baking powder (sodium bicarbonate), and in monosodium glutamate, a taste improver added to many processed and 'take-away' foods we buy. It is even used in the antacid drug preparations we obtain from the chemist shop.

To stay healthy as you get older, cut as much salt as possible out of your diet and try to get it to the adequate amount of up to four grams a day. Avoid foods with a high sodium content, such as those already mentioned. Steer clear of processed foods and eat more fresh fruit and vegetables, which are rich in potassium, sodium's complementary mineral. In your cooking, add less salt or none at all — it is surprising how people can adapt to the change by using other flavours such as herbs. Cut out using salt at the table by simply leaving the salt cellar in the cupboard. Alternatively use a salt cellar with some of the holes blocked off until you get used to the lack of salt, or use a salt substitute, available in chemists and health food stores.

Foods with a low-sodium content are fresh fruit and green vegetables, fruit juices, rice (if cooked without salt) flour, dried prunes, unsalted nuts and sugar — but you ought to cut down on sugar intake anyway. Look for muesli packs that state that no salt is added, or make your own. *Shredded Wheat* is about the only breakfast cereal that does not contain salt. Meat, milk, fresh fish, root vegetables, eggs, dried fruit, celery and pulses are the most beneficial foods that have a moderate sodium content.

## Selenium — a further clue to longevity

In recent years a lot of research has gone into the link between the trace element selenium and longevity. Scientists have discovered active old people well beyond their century, living in the Andes and other parts of the world, still cultivating their patch of selenium-rich soil. As a result, a lot has been written about the goodness of selenium in our lives and selenium is now available as a supplement. It works together with vitamin E in the body, and they are both powerful antioxidants. The supply of blood to the essential organs and tissue such as the skin and hair is dependent on adequate supplies of both vitamin E and selenium.

Selenium usually works by removing from the body the heavy metals such as lead and cadmium, which are responsible for so many of our diseases. A selenium deficiency impairs this process allowing the poisons to build up gradually in the system until illness occurs. It is believed that selenium prevents arthritis, cancer and heart disease if added to the diet regularly. Certainly, in areas such as the Andean region of South America where the soil is rich in selenium deposits, people live extremely long and active lives — although other factors, such as lifestyle, play their part in the causes of longevity.

Many soils are deficient in selenium as a result of the excessive use of fertilizers which contain too much sulphate. Modern food processing removes what little selenium is present — white bread and white sugar retain only a quarter of the amount of the mineral present in the raw material. It is thought that many of our diseases have occurred since so much selenium, along with other minerals, has been taken out of our diet. It is believed that lack of selenium reduces the efficiency of a particular enzyme so that body cells are less protected, and this is thought to be a factor in causing cancer. Studies have shown a relationship between selenium deficiency and certain types of cancer — and in certain areas of the world where selenium is severely lacking in the soil, cancer is prevalent.

It is certainly a good idea to eat foods richer in selenium, such as mushrooms, wholegrain cereals, nuts, vegetables, fruits, seafood, and offal (liver, kidneys and so on). It is also worthwhile taking a daily supplement of selenium to ensure against contracting the diseases of our Western world. A point to note in this country is that the area around Sheringham, Norfolk, which has the highest levels of selenium in the British Isles, has one of the oldest, most active communities in the country.

# 3

# The 'Wonder Foods' — Including Raw Juices

Certain foods have a direct influence on longevity, their devotees claim. Some advocate honey, others wheatgerm . . . as each food is given publicity, so a fashion for that particular food follows, for a while. Then there is a claim for another 'wonder food' and on it goes. Perhaps you should include a little of each in your diet, and see, if taken regularly, whether they make you feel healthier. First we should examine these foods — what do they contain and why are they supposed to be so necessary for a long healthy life?

Three of these 'wonder foods', yogurt, wheatgerm and brewer's yeast have an extremely important link — they are all rich sources of the B vitamins — the group we need to keep our nervous system ticking over smoothly. Without vitamin B we are in dire trouble. We feel lethargic easily, our skin shows blemishes and does not have a healthy glow, digestion is poor and bowel movements are irregular. With the B complex we have good appetite, good digestion, easy and regular bowel actions, plenty of energy, sound nerves, strong blood and good sight. There are many signs of B complex deficiency — wrinkled skin, poor eyesight, hair loss, greying hair, lack of energy, even anaemia. Deficiencies of this vitamin may lead to nervous disorders, skin trouble, heart problems, stomach ulcers, dyspepsia and constipation.

## Wheatgerm

Wheatgerm and brewer's yeast are the two best sources of the vitamin B complex. They have been labelled 'wonder foods', and some people have even claimed that they have been the greatest food discoveries of all time.

Wheatgerm contains vitamins $B_1$ (thiamin), $B_2$ (riboflavin), $B_6$ (pyridoxine), pantothenic acid, niacin, PABA, inositol and biotin — all B vitamins. Vitamin E and A are also present, together with twelve essential amino acids (proteins), and the minerals iron, phosphorus, potassium, magnesium, calcium, sodium and traces of several others.

Have a breakfast of two to four dessertspoonsful of wheatgerm — perhaps sprinkled over a favourite breakfast cereal or better still, a dish of muesli. It can also be taken separately with milk, followed by apricots or peaches, fresh or dried as available.

A grain of wheat is made up of three main parts. On the outside are layers of bran forming a protective fibrous coating. Beneath this is the endosperm, consisting mostly of starch. At the heart of the grain is the germ of the wheat, which is the living part that germinates when the grain is planted in the soil. At one time people did not need to think about their intake of wheatgerm because it was present in the bread they ate. In those days the whole grain could not be milled out of the flour. As milling techniques were refined in the nineteenth century, it became possible to mill the flour to a fine white powder, leaving out the rougher bran and wheatgerm grains. This type of flour became more fashionable and it was only the country people who perhaps milled their own flour who ate wholewheat flour and bread.

As a result, with a dearth of nutritional knowledge, the staple diet of the British people — and then the rest of the Western world — became extremely deficient. In recent years, however, wholewheat flour has made a comeback because doctors have discovered that so many ills of the Western world are caused by leaving out the goodness of the heart of the wheat and the bran layer. Bowel complaints, constipation, diverticular disease, cancer of the bowel, appendicitis, varicose veins and many more illnesses have been caused by the over-refined products we consume, the main culprits being the bland white bread and flour foods so much a part of our diet. White bread has only the starchy endosperm part of the grain left. Food manufacturers have been required by law to put back some of the vitamins lost during milling, but this law is soon to be lifted and so white bread will not even be as much of a food as it used to be.

You should eat some wholewheat bread every day, but as you get older it is a good idea to add some wheatgerm to other foods as well. This works particularly well if you find wholewheat bread a little heavy. One more point about bread. Brown bread is often confused with wholewheat bread, but in fact it is only white bread that has been coloured with caramel, and has none of the goodness of a wholewheat loaf.

Wheatgerm can be added to your cooking. Pastry cases can be made by mixing 8 oz (225g) wholewheat flour, one tablespoon wheatgerm, one tablespoon raw cane sugar, and 2 oz (55g) vegetable margarine together in a bowl and rubbing in with the fingers. Add water as necessary to bind the mixture together, then turn out and roll out flat. Line the pastry case, prick the base with a fork and then bake in a hot oven 400°F/200°C (Gas Mark 6) for 15-20 minutes. Then fill with the ingredients, savoury or sweet, of your choice.

For Wheatgerm Muffins mix together 1 tablespoon of vegetable margarine and 1 tablespoon of honey. In a bowl, mix 4 oz (115g) sifted wholewheat flour, 2 oz (55g) sifted soya flour, 4 oz (115g) wheatgerm, and ½ teaspoon baking powder. Add the honey mixture to the dry ingredients alternately with three quarters of a cup of yogurt. Beat it all together thoroughly, spoon into bun tins and bake for 35 minutes at 350°F/180°C (Gas Mark 4).

Try this recipe for Wholewheat Bread Rolls. Mix together ½ cup scalded milk, 2 oz (55g) vegetable margarine, a tablespoon of honey and a teaspoon of iodized vegetable salt. Cool this mixture by adding ½ cup water. Add 1 oz (30g) dried yeast, blend in a beaten egg, and finally add 1 lb (455g) wholewheat flour and two tablespoons of wheatgerm. Leave the mixture to rise in a warm place until it has doubled in bulk, divide and shape into rolls then bake for 20 minutes in a hot oven, 450°F/230°C (Gas Mark 8).

Add two or three tablespoons of wheatgerm to your favourite bread recipe, and add a tablespoonful whenever you make cakes. Sprinkle it over soups or salads. Make sure that you get a few spoonfuls of wheatgerm every day.

*Wheatgerm and vitamin E* Wheatgerm is the richest source of vitamin E, the vitamin that people need increasingly as they get older. Vitamin E has been found to be important in the prevention of heart disease and in treating infertility. It also tones up the muscles, prevents constipation and enriches the blood — so it is an important insurance against anaemia. It fights off potential heart conditions by making the muscles work with greater efficiency, which takes the strain off the heart. Without vitamin E the heart muscles need a larger amount of oxygen, causing breathlessness and heart strain. In some cases hardening of the arteries which carry the blood around the body to the heart, can be relieved by taking extra vitamin E.

Not only vitamin E but the B complex of vitamins, iron and vitamin C play their part in prolonging the life of the sex glands, but it has been found that deficiencies of vitamin E can have a great effect on the activity of the sex glands. It is essential for the health of both the ovaries in women and the male testicles. A loss of interest in sex in middle age can be blamed on too little vitamin E — a complete lack of it can even make men sterile. The early tests on laboratory rats in the 1920s revealed that the males, when deficient in vitamin E, became sterile, while the females, when given enough of the vitamin had normal births. As a result, vitamin E was increasingly seen as the wonder fertility vitamin — when in fact it has not turned out to be the panacea for all conditions connected with the sexual organs. It is more likely that vitamin E is just a link in the chain of biochemical reactions that makes a human being sexually active far into their life span. Certainly it should be taken with that in mind, in a balanced diet of natural wholegrain foods, fresh fruit and vegetables.

Studies in the USA have shown that treatment with vitamin E helped women with menopausal problems. Hot flushes, headaches and nervous symptoms were relieved and even eliminated in a study when 59 out of 66 women were successfully treated. They were given a daily dose of 100IU (international units) of the vitamin three times each day for three months. There are also many reports of women being relieved of the suffering caused by painful menstruation, and others with irregular periods have had their menstrual cycle made into a regular pattern once more. Heavy and scant menstrual flows are not influenced by the vitamin.

It is believed that vitamin E normalizes the blood levels of the oestrogens, the female sex hormones. The vitamin also improves the heat-regulating capacity of the body —

the reason for its success in controlling the hot flushes and excessive sweating experienced by many women during the menopause. Many doctors now think that it is safer to let the vitamin stimulate the body's own production of oestrogens as there is a risk in treating women with sex hormones especially when production starts to slow down in the menopause. By treating women with vitamin E during the menopause it is thought that the transition to and effects of decreased oestrogen production are made smoother and easier.

Vitamin E has also been very successfully used in treating many diabetic cases. Diabetes starts when the body can no longer control the level of blood sugar. Instead it has to be artificially controlled by the hormone insulin and various drugs taken orally. Later in life, however, other conditions can develop — kidney disease, high blood-pressure, heart problems, blindness, gangrene and neuritis. Studies of patients all over the world have shown that vitamin E, taken in large enough amounts, can prevent these conditions developing after middle age. Sometimes, where there has been an onset of such conditions treatment with the vitamin has cleared up the condition. Diabetics should take high doses of vitamin E only under the strict supervision of a qualified medical practitioner. The insulin dose may have to be decreased and the blood sugar level must be closely monitored for safety. As high a dose as 400IU of vitamin E has been stipulated to prevent these complications among diabetics — in certain treatments more may be necessary.

Skin complaints have been extremely successfully treated with vitamin E, which acts by stimulating the oxygen supply to the damaged skin. It is usually applied to the skin in an ointment or cream and afterwards the vitamin is given orally to help the body heal itself, quickly. Sunburn and skin damaged in accidents, including scalding, have been effectively treated with the vitamin. Dr Wilfred Shute, the eminent American authority on vitamin E, says that the vitamin lessens or removes the associated pain a few minutes after it is applied, and it also stops the burn from becoming deeper, limiting the damage to the cells actually destroyed by the burning agent. Lastly it makes new skin grow rapidly, leaving a small scar that is not painful. Leg ulcers which persist and are likely to become infected causing severe pain, have also responded well to vitamin E treatment. Again treatment consists of ointment and oral supplements.

Acne and eczema, not always confined to young people, and other skin blemishes, can be quickly cleared up with vitamin E ointment and oral tablets. Scar tissue caused by old blemishes which have left bluish tinges on the skin can be eradicated. The treatment is so effective it can be used on scar accident victims whose faces have been badly cut. In fact, many surgery units now use vitamin E ointment after operations in such cases as it is such a rapid, smooth healer with a mild antiseptic quality. There are many vitamin E creams on the market for general application to the skin to cover and heal scar tissue, not only to help the conditions already mentioned, but also to prevent ageing of the skin. Look around for neck and face creams with a vitamin E base, which should be applied at night and left on the skin. Some hand creams also contain vitamin E. Many other beauty products also state that they contain wheatgerm — the main source of the vitamin. Search for these, for they will be a good insurance against your skin showing signs of ageing.

## Brewer's Yeast

Dried brewer's yeast contains an even greater amount of valuable nutrients than wheatgerm, especially all the B group

## THE 'WONDER FOODS'

of vitamins, iron and phosphorus. It contains vitamin F (lecithin) which has a great effect on the blood as the red corpuscles consist of more than 50 per cent of this substance. Brewer's yeast contains sixteen amino acids (proteins), the body building foods, and other minerals including potassium, magnesium, silicon, copper, calcium, manganese and zinc.

No other foods contain such a long list of vitamins, minerals and amino acids as do these two foods, wheatgerm and brewer's yeast. They are therefore extremely important aids to keeping youthful looking in old age. Two teaspoons of brewer's yeast, taken in a glass of warm water in the evening before going to bed, will be enough to make a real difference in your health. There are other foods which also contain the B vitamins, of course, such as oats, wholewheat flour, brown rice, egg yolk, milk, apples, potatoes and tomatoes. These foods, however, don't contain the group of vitamins in nearly such concentrated amounts as are found in brewer's yeast, so purely as health insurance as you get older, it is of great benefit.

There are a variety of drinks that can be made with brewer's yeast to vary the monotony of taking yeast and water every day. Mix a small glass of natural yogurt with another small glass of tomato juice, and add a teaspoon of dried brewer's yeast. Alternatively mix a teaspoon of brewer's yeast into a glass of fresh grapefruit juice and stir well.

Add a teaspoonful of brewer's yeast to soup or vegetable stock for making soups or stews. Blend together a pint of tomato juice, a pint of natural yogurt, and two tablespoons of brewer's yeast. Add a pinch of salt substitute and blend all the ingredients until smooth — this makes an excellent breakfast drink.

This drink is an excellent appetizer. Mix two tablespoons brewer's yeast with a pint of tomato juice, a few squeezes of lemon juice to taste and some chopped chives or parsley. Shake until the drink is frothy. Store in the fridge if you don't use it straight away.

## Yogurt

The last two 'wonder foods' in this group will need no introduction — they are as popular now as they were in the days of the Bible, although in somewhat different form and presentation. They are yogurt and honey.

Firstly, yogurt. Rich in the B group of vitamins, as are wheatgerm and brewer's yeast, it is found in all shops nowadays and in many flavours. To tempt young palates, even yogurt drinks in fruit flavours are now available. It is natural yogurt — especially the home-made variety — that will do you the most good. It can, of course, have fruit or nuts added to it but steer clear of sugar. Commercial yogurt, even though it may be well within its sell by date, will almost certainly have started to deteriorate as it will be several days old. Yogurt should be eaten as fresh as possible to get the maximum benefit from it. You cannot tell when a shop-bought yogurt was actually made and after a week the beneficial bacteria present in it will have started to deteriorate. If you cannot make it at home yourself — and it really is a simple process, needing no cooking — try to make sure that you buy it from a farm or a person who makes it at home. Health food stores usually sell locally-made yogurt too. That way you will be getting a fresher product and one that will do you more good.

Yogurt is supposed to have been first made by the nomadic tribes of Eastern Europe. We all know that fresh milk turns sour after a time, especially if it is kept at a warm temperature. Its organisms convert some of the lactose (otherwise known as milk sugar) present in the milk into lactic acid. A lactic fermentation takes place and the milk becomes yogurt. It is still made in this way in the Middle East and the Balkan regions. In the Western world yogurt is made by adding yogurt culture to warm milk. The rather grand name for a very simple process is inoculation. The organism which turns milk into yogurt is *lactobacillus bulgaricus*.

Yogurt is favoured by nutritionalists because it has a natural antibiotic quality and can kill off harmful bacteria in the intestines. It contains iron, calcium, vitamins A, $B_1$, niacin, a little vitamin C, linoleic acid, phosphorus and potassium. Lastly, and very importantly as you get older, it is more easily digested than milk, because of the lactic acid it possesses. It is fair to say that people with a poor digestion probably exist on an inadequate diet in the first place. If you are prone to heartburn or similar discomfort then milk will only add to the problems, coagulating in the stomach, causing indigestion. Yogurt will not have this effect. Although yogurt has the same food value as milk, the casein in milk which causes it to become a solid mass in the stomach and therefore sometimes indigestible, has been broken down when it is turned into yogurt, so it becomes instantly more digestible. Yogurt is very good for people who need extra protein but cannot assimilate foods in other forms — people recovering from an illness, for example. It will also help the stomach to digest the other proteins. Yogurt helps ease constipation and gastric irritation. If a person is constipated they must have a fibre-filled diet and yogurt will help the stomach get used to the more fibrous foods as well as activate the bowels easily.

Yogurt and similar fermented foods have been made all over the world for centuries, using whatever animal milk is available, cow's or goat's milk being the most popular. Sheep milk yogurt is becoming increasingly available in this country on a local basis. An angel is supposed to have told Abraham the way to make yogurt, and as he lived to be 175 and became a father for the umpteenth time as he turned a century, the idea of yogurt giving a fertile long life has grown up for a very long time indeed. The ancient Greeks wrote about the health-giving properties of yogurt. They believed it was particularly good for digestive upsets and for regulating the intestinal tract, and they were right. Yogurt was not so well known in the Western world, where other fermented milk products such as curds and whey, and junket, formed the basis of milk foods. But over the past few years a gap emerged as interest in making junkets and similar milky foods declined, and this gap came to be filled with commercially-produced cartons of yogurt. One of the reasons for the interest in natural yogurt was the longevity of the Bulgarian people who rely so strongly on it in their diet. Naturally, other factors must be taken into account, but the longevity of people who include yogurt in their daily food is interesting to anyone who wants to stay youthful long past their middle years.

It is extremely simple to make your own yogurt. You will find many electric yogurt makers in the shops but they are not essential. You can make your own delicious yogurt in a bowl then set it aside to ferment in a warm place. You will need a starter for the first batch — either some natural yogurt or yogurt culture, which can be obtained from a health food store and must be unflavoured. The milk must also be pasteurized so that there are no alien bacteria to combat the beneficial bacteria which turn the milk into yogurt. A food thermometer is a good idea when you are new to making yogurt, but again not essential. Bring the milk to just above body temperature (43°C/110°F), just comfortable if you test it with a clean finger. If you use cow's milk it must be boiled first, then cooled down to the right temperature. Sometimes cows are given antibiotics which, if not driven off by boiling, can fight the lactobacillus bacteria and prevent the yogurt setting. Goat's milk need not be boiled first.

Let the milk simmer at the low temperature for a while — up to three quarters of an hour on a very slow ring, or just stand it on the cooker for that time while the oven is on. Make sure it is the correct heat then add it to the starter which should have been placed in the bowl first. Stir it well to activate the starter, then cover with a clean cloth and leave in a warm place for several hours, or overnight. A warm kitchen or an airing cupboard is ideal. Yogurt is also very successfully made in a wide-necked vacuum flask — and one of the yogurt makers on the market is based on this idea. It does not really need to be covered with a cloth unless there is a draught coming into the room.

The longer you leave the milk on the stove, and the longer you leave it fermenting in the bowl or flask, the thicker the yogurt will be. After you have made one batch, keep a little back as a starter for the next one — and make sure that it is not too old. The best idea is to make a pint or so of fresh yogurt every day or two. The amount of yogurt used as a starter can be as little as a teaspoon, or even a trace of yogurt will do, if the conditions are right. Often people advise using one or two tablespoons as a starter, but really this is a waste. On the whole, it is easier to use cow's milk for yogurt, especially when you are a beginner. Cow's milk is easier to set than goat's milk, although goat's milk is delicious and has a flavour all of its own. Skimmed milk, soya milk — all can be made into yogurt. A thicker yogurt can be obtained by adding skimmed milk powder to the mixture at the beginning of the process. Use about one level teaspoon to one pint of milk.

Use your yogurt in a variety of ways. It is delicious and very nutritious added to muesli for breakfast or as a snack at any time of the day. It can also be used in place of cream — with far less fat — as a more healthy topping for puddings and desserts. For instance, it is delicious over a wholewheat fruit crumble. Add yogurt to casseroles and stir it into soups — but take care never to boil or overheat it as it will separate. Just heat it through gently and watch it all the time. Add yogurt to cheese sauces just before serving.

Make your own healthy yogurt dressing to make a change from salad oil and mayonnaise — and again a healthier alternative. Mix natural yogurt with lemon juice, chives and pepper. It is especially good with apple and nut salad mixtures. Yogurt and thinly sliced cucumber is a popular Eastern side dish — good with other salads or to cool down a hot curry.

Stir a fresh fruit purée into natural yogurt to make a fruit fool. Add chopped nuts and a little honey if you prefer. There are so many ways to serve this healthy and versatile food that you need never get bored with it.

## Honey

More controversy abounds over this food than probably any other — certainly more than any for which a 'wonder food' claim has been made. There are, on the one hand, the devotees who insist that honey will cure all or most of our ills and give us longevity and vitality. Then there is the large band of doctors and nutritionists who see honey purely as a food loaded with sugar and as potentially dangerous as any other sugar, even though it is a natural food. It is then, a food which you must learn about and then weigh up all the arguments. Certainly too much honey will cause obesity and illness just as an excess of any sugar will. Having said that, honey has some special properties and should form part of a healthy balanced diet.

Honey is a natural antiseptic which can kill bacteria. It contains many of the B vitamins and folic acid, and it can contain large quantities of vitamin C. Some of the vitamins may be lost in filtering the honey. A whole list of vitamins are in the food — iron, copper, sodium, manganese, potassium, magnesium, phosphorus and calcium. There are amino and other acids, enzymes and of course natural sugars. Generally speaking the darker the honey, the more nutritious components will be present. To make sure that the honey you buy has not been darkened artificially buy it from a good health food store or other reputable source. It is only fair to add that honey is composed of 75 per cent sugars and 17 per cent water, the rest being made up of the nutrients listed above — so they are not present in very large amounts. However, they are all in a valuable combination.

Honey is the best natural sweetener, not only because of these valuable nutrients, but also because of the very important fact that it is already digested by the bee and so the body can put it to instant use as an energy giver. The nectar collected by the bee is composed of several types of sugars which are converted by the bees into simple sugars, called levulose and dextrose, which can be absorbed straight into the blood-stream. So it is also good for people with digestive problems, for it neutralizes acid. As it is so easily absorbed into the blood-stream, it is a boost for anyone who needs extra energy for work or sport. Obviously to take honey in excess of your energy needs means that fat stores will accumulate and you will put on weight — so take honey in moderation as and when you need it.

All aspects of the life of the bee in the hive have been studied and put to use by country people through the centuries. Honey itself has been regarded as a cure-all, for everything from arthritis to bed-wetting. Honeycomb, when chewed, is supposed to relieve hay fever symptoms. Due to its antiseptic qualities, honey is used as an ointment for minor burns, cuts and to heal scars. Royal jelly, the jelly-like honey which the bees make to feed their young queen, is believed to be the secret of eternal youth. Native people all over the world use this substance to keep their skin youthful and wrinkle-free. It is certainly rich in hormones and enzymes, and many commercial brands of royal jelly cream or tablets can be obtained from health food stores.

Propolis is another by-product of the bee hive. It is the substance made by the bees themselves to keep the hive glued together. It is sold in shops in liquid and tablet form and also as a healthier alternative to ordinary sweets, but of course with the same risk to teeth.

Pollen itself is collected from the hive, treated and manufactured into tablets which are often used by sportsmen for their energy-giving qualities during training.

Honey should be taken as a daily tonic in a glass of warm water. As much as a couple of tablespoons taken in a glass either two hours before or after a meal will be most beneficial, and this can be repeated three times a day (only if you don't take honey in another way during the day — be careful about this, or you will have a weight problem). For colds, take honey and cider vinegar in equal amounts in half a cup of warm water. This will also soothe a sore throat. Or take a tablespoon of honey, another of glycerine, a dessertspoon of lemon juice and a little ginger. Honey in lemon juice and water or honey simply added to warm milk is a good bedtime drink whether you have a cold or not because the calcium in the milk induces sleep.

Although honey gives energy it also has a sedative effect.

It can be very helpful for people who are tense and nervous and who suffer from insomnia. It also has a slightly laxative effect, but a gentle one. Other illnesses that are helped by taking honey are anaemia, kidney problems, liver complaints, eye troubles, heart illnesses, arthritis and rheumatism. It is good for skin problems too — although a rather sticky alternative to the usual preparations. See Chapter 5, Health and Beauty, for details.

When you examine the various honey jars in shops you will see how many shades and types there are. So many factors make up a particular type of honey — the flowers the bees gather their nectar from, the climate, the season of the year. Some plants give more nectar at certain times of the year. It is fascinating to real all the labels — clover honey, acacia honey, heather honey and so on, and also to note their country or locality of origin. Don't buy a honey that is a product of more than one country — it cannot be pure. Another point to bear in mind is that some cheaper brands are inferior because the bees are fed on a solution of sugar that is positioned at the hive entrance and so the natural enzyme action does not take place.

Store honey in a dry place that is not too cold. It will darken with age and the taste will probably get stronger. If it crystallizes it is either rather old or is in a place that is too damp. You can stand the honey jar in a pan of warm water and heat it through gently. Use honey in your cooking instead of sugar. In baking use three quarters the amount of sugar stated in the recipe and reduce the liquid by one-fifth for each half cup of honey used.

### Raw Juices

One of the quickest ways to give yourself instant energy, especially if you are rather jaded, is to drink a glass of freshly-pressed vegetable or fruit juice, not the supermarket carton kind, but fresh from your garden preferably, or the best local source of produce you can find — from organically-grown fruits or vegetables, if possible. Raw juices release vitamins and minerals to the body straight away and within a few minutes they are pumping around in your blood-stream. Nutrition experts like the late Gayelord Hauser recommend people of all ages, but particularly those over forty, to take a pint of raw juice each day. Just as cooking destroys so much natural goodness, by juicing vegetables and fruits you will be releasing all the nutrients in a way that the body finds easy to assimilate. No one would want to eat a plateful of raw carrots, but when they are juiced they become easy to digest even for people with digestive problems. They are ideal for convalescents and older people — but they are also good for people of all ages, and will help to guard against future illness.

Young plants, full of energy from the sun, soil, air and water surrounding them, are the best type of juice. Green leaved vegetables should be dark green, carrots should not be yellow but dark orange (thus containing more vitamin A), apples shold be crisp and juicy, not mushy and bruised. Select only the best fruit and vegetables available. Don't soak them in water, or the vitamins will run out into the soaking water, but just scrub them and use them quickly. Don't peel carrots and other root vegetabls — much of their goodness lies just under the skin. Celery should be tender and not old looking. Cut the produce up small enough to go into the juicer. Citrus fruits can be easily pressed by an ordinary squeezer, although there are several good types of electric citrus presses on the market.

Sip your juice slowly, or it may cause some discomfort. Take more than a pint a day only if you are being supervised by a nutritionist. Add a few drops of lemon or orange juice to improve the flavour, and honey if you really dislike the taste of fresh juice. Mix flavours — carrot juice can be mixed with all the other juices, and so can celery. The dark green vegetables such as spinach need the addition of carrot or some other milder tasting vegetable to take off the rather sharp taste — equal parts of celery, carrot and spinach are a good combination.

Cabbage juice is one that has had many claims made for it, especially after a doctor in California, Dr Cheney, found that it cured his patients of ulcers within a fortnight. They were given all cabbage juice, or three parts cabbage juice mixed with one part celery juice, at various times throughout the day, a total of 16 fl oz (450 ml) each day. Cabbage should be picked young and tender for sweet light tasting juice — just add a bit of celery or some dark leaves of cabbage for extra flavour. Large quantities of cabbage juice should not be taken for long periods as it can cause, in excessive amounts, a thyroid complaint and make a goitre in the neck. However, taken regularly in small amounts with other vegetables, it will treat many disorders and infections of the digestive system.

Both apple and tomato juices are delicious enough to be drunk on their own, although they can be mixed with other flavours. Don't peel the ripe tomatoes, but just drop them in the juicer, and add a dash of lemon juice to the drink — as well as being so good for you, with vitamins A, C and some B, tomato juice is a marvellous appetizer. Apple juice is a great cleanser for the systems and is a blood purifier, good for the skin and the liver. It is full of vitamins A, B and C (although varying with different varieties), and many minerals.

All the citrus juices, especially pineapple, are very good and a great boost for the system. Pineapple is very kind to the digestion and contains the A, B and C vitamins, besides nine minerals including iodine. So although pineapples are expensive, treat yourself to a glass or two of juice whenever you can.

Cucumbers are a great tonic for sufferers of rheumatism. The juice is very high in potassium, other minerals and the vitamins A, B and C. Do not peel the cucumbers, just cut them up into strips before processing. Mix the juice with apple, carrot or celery juice as it needs a lift in flavour.

Rhubarb supposedly contains a substance which helps to protect the teeth which is surprising in such a strong-tasting plant. Rhubarb is excellent for the complexion, especially if mixed with fresh young strawberries. It makes a beautiful summery drink, and it can be sweetened with some honey. Float some sprigs of mint on the top and you have a lovely summer cocktail.

Grape juice is another famous health drink, drunk in health spas in Europe where people take the Grape Cure regularly. Apart from its vitamin content — A, B and C — plus many minerals, the large amount of inert sugar in grapes makes it ideal for slimming diets, giving energy without being fattening.

Two of the least likely juices are watercress and parsley, but these should be added to other juices, for they contain valuable amounts of nutrients. Parsley is the richest source of vitamin A among vegetables, and should not be confined to garnishing dishes of food. It is also high in other vitamins, especially vitamin C and contains a small quantity of vitamin E. Its minerals include iron — so add some to your other vegetable drinks. Watercress is rich in all the minerals, especially iodine, but it is rather bitter and too strong to be used on its own. Mix it with other juices; with cucumber to relieve rheumatism; with carrot and spinach for anaemia,

## THE 'WONDER FOODS'

or just diluted with spring water as a general spring clean for the system. This can be taken in very small amounts throughout the day. It purifies, strengthens the blood, helps the digestive system, the gall bladder and the liver.

Practically any fruit or vegetables, with the exception of garlic and horseradish, can be put through a juicer. Don't store the juice for too long — make it fresh each day if you can, and keep it in the fridge. Make cocktails for yourself and for your friends from mixtures — try apple and apricot juice in equal amounts, or apple and grape juice, apple and pear juice, strawberry and apricot juice, grapefruit and pineapple juice, or for a more savoury appetizer, three parts tomato juice and one part of celery juice. There are many more combinations you can try out for yourself. Serve them attractively in glasses with a slice of lemon or other citrus fruit and sprigs of mint floating on the top. Even in the winter they can give a taste of summer, evocative, relaxing and health giving.

# 4

# Exercise

Don't sit back in that chair reading this book! Well, wait until you've read this chapter . . . and then get going. The worst thing you can do is to think that because you are a certain age that you must take life easy. On the contrary, you need to exercise your body and your brain or you will age before your time. The more people sit around the more tired they feel. Imagine going to bed for a fortnight. At the end of it you would not feel energetic and rested, but lethargic and weak. Your muscles would lose their tone, through lack of use. You would feel irritable instead of relaxed.

One of the leading American figures on the health scene for the past ten years or so was the late Gayelord Hauser, who said: 'There is no good reason why people should tire more easily as they grow older. Constant fatigue is not normal at any age. I believe that it is caused largely by dietary deficiencies and extensive scientific experiments (both with animals and human volunteers) have shown this to be so'.

He cited the example of the young nurses at the famous Mayo Clinic who offered to be 'guinea pigs' in an experiment. Instead of eating fresh vegetables and proteins they embarked on what he called a typical 'Old Ladies' Home Diet' of cooked-to-death vegetables, devitalized starches, white bread, white sugar and gooey pastries. After a time they found themselves irritable instead of good-natured, listless instead of energetic. The whole thing ran in a vicious circle. The more tired they became, the more they ate, trying to regain some of their usual energy. But as they ate more of this sort of food, the more listless and fatigued they became. Gayelord Hauser maintained that people who eat fresh, natural foods stay fitter and less tired. Research has shown that the 'rest home' type of diet (which is hopefully not found in many such homes these days), is lacking in the ever vital B group of vitamins. We need these vitamins for energy and without them we become jumpy, irritable and extremely tired.

After putting your diet to rights (see Chapter 2) you must put your body to work, but in a relaxing way. Relaxation is the key word here. It has been said that tension is age, relaxation is youthfulness. Imagine that you are extremely cross with someone — you may find that very easy. You will feel your body tense up, your mouth will harden, your eyes will narrow. All those facial contortions cause lines and eventually, wrinkles and the hard faces seen in many older people. If you feel tense all the time, your body never has the chance to relax. The best way you can combat tension and its ageing effects in your life is to learn to relax completely. Complete relaxation is an art, one which expectant mothers are taught, and yoga teachers demonstrate. It is difficult to just let everything go and make your mind a blank, but that is what you must try and achieve — so practise it.

There are a whole range of relaxation techniques — choose the one you enjoy the most. Apart from yoga, there are exercise routines, meditation, massage, water therapy which tackles stress through baths, saunas and wrapping treatments.

There is even autogenics, in which the person goes through a series of easy mental exercises based on auto- or self-suggestion. They have been found to slow down the heart rate and to produce similar effects to those of meditation. Autogenics is a fairly easy type of mental exercise to follow, and can be practised quietly at home. The technique was thought up by Dr J. H. Schultz, a German neurologist. In a sequence of instructions made to yourself, you focus in a meditating fashion, which makes you aware of particular areas of the body. There's no effort involved, just concentrate on the emotions or sensations caused by each exercise.

Do the exercises in a comfortable position, sitting in a quiet room that is free of distractions. It's a good idea to practice twice each day, and allow a two hour gap after meals. Try to give yourself twenty minutes for each exercise session. Begin by repeating to yourself several times, 'I am relaxed and at peace with myself'. Follow this with a sequence of exercises, starting with your right arm. Focus mentally on it, and say, 'My right arm is heavy'. After a few minutes, repeat the phrase several times, then go on to the left arm, right leg then left leg, neck, shoulders and back. Each exercise should take half to one minute.

The second exercise uses the words 'My right arm (or whatever part of the body you are focusing on) is warm'. Repeat this a few times, then proceed in the same way as for the first exercise. Pause for a few seconds to see if there are any sensations apparent, which are more likely to be felt when the mind is passive and receptive.

The third exercise focuses on the breathing cycle using the words, 'My breathing is calm and regular'. Don't try and control breathing, just repeat the phrase slowly again and again which will make your breathing deep, slow and regular without any effort. Then repeat the phrase, 'My forehead is cool', for several minutes — the effect of this is to both relax the mind and make it alert as well. The last phrase to be used is 'I am alert and refreshed', which should be repeated for a minute or so. Then breathe deeply, stretch yourself throughout the body as a cat does after a nap, and you should be refreshed enough to meet the demands of the rest of the day.

Some people may need to go through a short training course in autogenics and they should find a properly qualified instructor. There are other exercises directed at the heart beat and the solar plexus and these really must be supervised by a qualified person, because they can produce adverse affects such as a rise in blood-pressure. But the simple exercises outlined above have helped people with many stress-related disorders, such as migraine, high blood-pressure, asthma, insomnia, nervous sweating and skin troubles. There are many forms of massage and therapies — many of them available at health clubs and by qualified practitioners. Yoga classes abound and, of course, by going to a class you'll make new contacts and friends.

The best and easiest ways of feeling younger and looking more youthful are to breathe more deeply, and develop good posture. Nothing ages a person more than stooping hunched shoulders and a permanently curved spine. Start with posture — that's essential! Your ribs won't be able to expand and you won't be able to fill your lungs with air unless you stand up straight and tall. If you slouch, you only use your upper chest for breathing which becomes shallow, causing stress and tension. Short, panting breath is only for emergencies such as after running, when the muscles have used up their oxygen supply. If you always breathe in this way the body is put under a lot of pressure.

Yoga is excellent for practising deep breathing — so is

singing. Keep breathing evenly, standing tall with your shoulders back. Lelord Kordel says this about posture: 'You can improve your posture . . . without violent exercise. Try standing tall, pulling in your abdomen, and holding your chin up. Good posture is directly related to your feeling of self-respect.' He goes to give this exercise for creating good posture. 'Draw the abdomen in vigorously as far as possible, then exhale. A stooping posture decreases the efficiency of the heart and lungs and injures the work of the liver. If you'll repeat this exercise several times daily you'll strengthen the muscles that hold your abdomen in place.' This exercise can easily be carried out during the day, at home or at the office. It only takes a few seconds and it can achieve so much in terms of well-being.

Then, having relaxed a little and improved your posture considerably (just keep remembering not to slouch), try some simple exercises that again can be fitted into the routine of your day. Everyone can do a bit more stretching, bending and reaching without straining, and instead they will be helping themselves to keep supple. The Royal Canadian Air Force suggest in their exercise booklet that people balance on one foot while putting their shoes and socks on. So simple! Or try sitting on the floor, raising both legs in the air and balancing your bottom while putting on socks or tights. If it's done properly you will form a V shape with your legs in the air and you'll feel your leg, back and abdominal muscles getting some very good exercise at the same time. How about polishing the floor with a duster and your behind? Many people know about this exercise — sit on the floor and walk across with your bottom — it's very good for reducing that problem area around the bottom, especially for pear-shaped British women. It's easier on a shiny floor, so polishing it at the same time will be a bit of an incentive!

There are 700 voluntary muscles of all sizes in the human body. These are the muscles that have to be worked — the others, the involuntary muscles, work automatically, so they need not to be worried about. It's the other 700 we've got to work at. They are used when we stand, walk, jog, bend, stretch — every activity you can think of. They are not used when we are sitting down — unless you are practising some isometric exercises. Doctors urge us to wiggle and move all the muscles we can more often, and these exercises, however small, can be effective not only for the body but also for the brain. Brain surgeons have advised people to exercise their muscles more, not only to improve their circulation and help the heart to pump blood to the brain, but also to stop other faculties from deteriorating. Even wiggling your toes can be beneficial. You'll be doing a service to your heart and brain and the rest of you. Keep your arms and legs moving for the same reason — otherwise, you'll start to see the ageing signs of defective eyesight, hearing and mental faculties.

Isometric exercises became popular because they can be done at home and need only take a short time each day. It is important to do them consistently — once a week, even for an hour, is no good. The vital thing to remember is to exercise each day, even for a couple of minutes. Try and build up to more of an exercise programme but don't be over-ambitious. That way you are less likely to fall down on your goals.

Isometric exercises are those in which you tense one set of muscles against another, or against some strong immoveable object such as a wall or table. Most of them can be done sitting down at a desk or table or just by standing up and moving over to the wall or kitchen sink. That's why they became so popular. The desk-bound sections of the US

Marines were given these exercises and found that within twenty weeks they doubled the strength of the muscles they exercised. Remember that isometrics can't take the place of more violent exercise which carries oxygen to the blood-stream and stimulates the circulation, but they can be of great benefit. If you do have problems with circulatory disorders or respiratory troubles then get advice from a doctor before embarking on these or any form of exercise. Due to a reflex action beyond voluntary control, strong contractions can stop the blood circulating.

*For the waist and abdomen*
Also called the 'stomach lift', this is one of the best known and most widely practised isometric exercises. It can be done anywhere and you can do it sitting, standing or lying down — it's up to you. Simply tighten the abdominal muscles, contracting them as hard as you can. Try to feel your stomach being pulled right back to your backbone. Hold it like that for a few seconds, or until the muscles start to shake a little with the tension, and relax. This exercise is obviously popular because it can be done so easily at any time and doesn't need much thinking about. Get into the habit of doing an exercise like this quite often throughout the day.

*For the abdomen, arms, legs and thighs*
Sitting well back on a chair, hold your legs straight out and place the palms of your hands above the knees. Press downwards with your arms and upwards with your legs, making the resistance strongly felt.

*Ankle flex*
Try to flex the foot (either sitting or standing) upwards from the ankle joint. You can form the resistance needed with your hands or some other object. This is good for the lower leg muscles.

# EXERCISE

## Chest and arms
This exercise both firms and strengthens the chest and arms and it is good for both men and women, firming up flabby chests and giving the bust a boost. Bend your arms in front of the chest, lock your fingers together and hold the palms of the hands together at the same time. Press hard and hold like that until the pectoral muscles (the chest muscles) quiver with the tension caused by the exercise.

## Arms and neck
Put the left hand palm against the left side of the head. Press against the hand with the head. Do this exercise again on the right hand side, the front and the back of the head. If you suffer from weak neck muscles this exercise will help strengthen them.

## Shoulders, chest and arms (standing)
Stand in the middle of a doorway, with your feet apart. Place your hands against the sides of the doorway so that they are at shoulder height. Your arms should be bent. Press hard with the palms against the doorway sides.

## Shoulders, chest and arms (sitting)
While you are sitting down, grasp the arms of the chair firmly, then lift hard for a few seconds, as if you were trying to pull them up to your shoulders. As an alternative, you can press down on the chair arms just as hard as you can for a few seconds.

## Upper back and arms
Stand about a foot or a bit more away from a wall, your back facing the wall. With the arms alongside the body, place the palms against the wall. Keep the arms straight, and try to push against the wall — as though you were trying to push it down.

There are various other isometric exercises, using different sets of muscles. They should be used in addition to the above exercises, not as a replacement for them. You should combine these exercises with the more vigorous type such as jogging or aerobics, or even brisk walking, dancing or a racket sport.

Isometrics will not stimulate the circulation, fill your lungs with oxygen or help to stop fatty deposits building up in the arteries. More vigorous exercise will do that — isometrics merely strengthen, tone and firm up the muscles. Some experts claim that the muscles built up by isometrics are of no use when people want to apply strength, and that isometrics won't help endurance.

Another warning — there is a piece of exercise equipment which you may come across, called the *Bullworker*. It is designed on isometric principles and it does strengthen and form the muscles. But if you are a little, or more than a little, hypertensive, avoid this type of exercise machine as it can put stress on the heart and make your blood-pressure rise. On the other hand, if you don't suffer in that way, the *Bullworker* is the most efficient isometric machine in that it encourages resistance progressively, by making it easy to measure how your strength is improving. As your strength increases, movement becomes harder.

There is no way that you can cheat at getting fit. Exercise machines are just an aid — you must do the work yourself. Vibrator belts, for instance, can be good for toning up muscles, but only when used alongside more demanding exercise. When you go to gyms, leisure centres or health clubs you will find many types of isotonic exercise machines. These are based on weight training principles. Whereas in isometrics the muscles contract without any movement at the joints, in isotonic exercises the muscle work with the joints as well. The most common machines work on the dumb-bell and barbell method. They are easier to handle than hand-held devices, and so are safer to use. They can isolate special muscle groupings for intensive training and so people can manage heavier weights with them.

Its always a good idea to train in a club or gym rather than buy an exercise machine, even a jogging, cycling or rowing machine for home use. To start with, the staff at a club or gym can help and supervise and should be trained to act if anyone is in difficulties. It's also more fun in a group and you are less likely to stop using the machine — too many of these are bought for home use and after the initial novelty has worn off, gather dust like so many of the gadgets people buy.

Exercise bicycles are geared to improving heart and lung fitness and they strengthen the leg muscles. You can increase the resistance as you get stronger, by using a brake on the wheel or pedals. These machines are usually calibrated so that the work rate can be measured, and sometimes they have a heart-rate monitor and a calorie counter to show how much energy has been used. Rowing machines strengthen the arms, shoulders and back. The feet of the 'rower' are fixed by a strap at the front, and the sliding seat exercises the legs in bending and pushing movements. Jogging machines usually look like a modern version of the treadmill, motorized and with rails to hold on to. They benefit the heart and lungs. They can be adjusted to various speeds for different levels of fitness. The lat machine strengthens and shapes the back muscles and the muscles at the backs of the upper arms. A bar which is on a cable attached to weights via a pulley is grasped and pulled down. Different grips work on the different areas of the back. If you are planning to take a skiing holiday, the twist board is a good way of toning up the body in preparation. It strengthens the waist and the leg muscles.

It can be either a single, or double model, for use by one or two people at a time. You stand on the disc and push against the fixed T-bar to the right and to the left, keeping the feet stationary and straight.

## Water Exercises

Swimming — and any exercise in water — is one of the very best ways to keep fit. The resistance of water helps to build up body strength while at the same time the buoyancy of water supports the weight of the body. All the muscles of the body are used while swimming and people of any age can manage to swim for at least a short way, and enjoy water exercise, which will leave them feeling refreshed. Many older people have learnt to swim and this gives a great sense of achievement and youthfulness. There are special courses for mature beginners available at local swimming pools.

Exercising in water particularly helps people with back, knee, hip or ankle problems, because most of them are practised in water that is chest deep and there is usually a hand rail to hold on to for support. For non-swimmers these exercises help to build up confidence in the water and are good to do if you are a parent keeping an eye on your children in the water. Water is a good medium to exercise in because its buoyancy relieves the pressure of gravity on the spine and gives the muscles at the back of the body and legs a chance to relax. Muscles often feel stiff and heavy because of the waste products, built up by tension in the blood-stream. Water movements involve less tension, so they are good ways to relax.

One exercise that helps the spine to stretch out and relax is this: with your hands on the rail at the side of the pool, lie prone in the water. Keep your knees straight and relax your ankles, then kick with your legs. Don't kick too hard, just about a foot away is enough. Try to manage about a dozen or more kicks. This can also be done lying on your back although some people may find it hard to manage as they won't be able to float easily. Floating is not as easy as many of us think — it has a lot to do with the body weight distribution and the shape of the body — so don't be disheartened if you find it difficult. There are other exercises you can try. The good thing about this exercise, though, is that it helps to slim the thighs, reduces the tensions and pain that go with arthritic conditions, and as it also relaxes the ankles it can help prevent ankle injuries.

The following exercise is to help lose some of that flab on the upper arms. It is best done at the deep end as it strengthens the arms more if you can push with your feet. With your back to the edge, hold the rail fairly close to the body. Then straighten your arms to lift your weight upwards. Hold for a second like this before moving down, and try to repeat this eight times. Even people with weak arms can do this because the water holds you up.

This exercise slims the buttocks and thighs, and it stretches the inside thigh muscles. Stand facing the pool side and hold the rail with both hands. Swing your right leg behind you, then bring it forwards as if jumping a hurdle, bending the knee, but keeping the thigh in a line with the floor of the pool. With your leg make circles back to the starting position, and repeat eight times to one side and eight to the other.

Try this exercise for slimming the waist, strengthening the arms, and making your neck and spine more mobile. Stand close to the edge of the pool, face sideways and hold the rail with your left hand. Turn your head to the right and stretch your right arm outwards. Then lean right out from the rail, straightening your left arm but still remembering to keep your feet by the edge of the pool. Stretch your right hand up and arch your body over to the left. Repeat the exercise eight times to each side.

An excellent way of slimming the outside of the thighs and waist, to reduce a double chin, and at the same time make the arms more supple and the chest open up, is this simple exercise. Stand on your right leg in the water. Then lift your left leg straight up to the side, to make it on a line with the surface of the water. Stretch your arms right out to the sides to help you balance, and turn your head to the left to tone up the muscles in your neck. Hold like that for three seconds, then repeat four times to each side.

Try this last exercise to slim and strengthen your abdomen and thigh muscles, and to make your spine more mobile. Stand away from the poolside, then clasp your hands behind your head. Lift your left knee up and bring the right elbow down to meet it. Repeat with the right knee and left elbow. Try this five times each leg. This is an exercise which can be done at home — it doesn't need water, but of course the medium of water makes it an even more useful muscle strengthener and body trimmer.

As you try these exercises more often you will find that they become easier which shows the muscles are working more and firming up. Try not to rest too long between exercises — and this goes for any exercise — because your body will cool down, stop being so relaxed and start to stiffen again. The idea is to keep moving. You may feel a bit stiff the day after you've first tried these exercises — or if there has been a long gap between visits to the pool. Try to go as often as you can and the feeling of stiffness will wear off — the reason for this feeling is that the water's resistance is greater than it seems at the time. In between your visits to the pool, keep up with bending and stretching exercises at home, perhaps to music. They do not have to be vigorous — but enough to make you still feel supple.

## Aerobics

We hear so much about aerobics these days — it conjures up mental pictures of young girls in bright leotards cavorting around to loud and frantic pop music in a way that would send many forty-plus people off to the nearest armchair. But aerobics does not have to be like that.

The word 'aerobic' means 'with oxygen'. This idea of getting the pulse to race and giving the body more energy can be equally found in many sports. Jogging, running, swimming, a brisk up-hill walk, cycling, skipping, even cross country skiing, all have the same effect. It just happens that aerobic dancing is the fashion at the moment.

Like many fashionable pastimes, aerobics has soared so quickly in popularity that people have gone into it without a lot of thought and now there is a backlash of opinion against it from the medical profession and qualified fitness instructors. Many classes are being started by girls who look good in a leotard and can probably manage the routines themselves with ease but who have no teaching qualifications and insufficient expertise to see if anything is going wrong in their classes. They are not usually trained in first aid so can be of little help if someone has an injury or collapses in their session. As a result, there have been many injuries, mainly to the spine, and often these are not easily treated. So if you do decide to take up aerobic dancing — and it is great fun — check on the qualifications of the instructor. Go and watch the class. See if there is adequate warming up and cooling down at the start and end of each session, so that muscles are fully relaxed and less prone to injury. Watch the instructor to see if she or he is on the look out for anyone hurting themselves. Join the class only when you are satisfied that it is up to standard.

In a good aerobic dance class, each set of the body muscles

is worked on in turn. Floor mats help to ease any discomfort, especially if the floor is not too good. The warm-up is very important — keep your leg warmers, ankle warmers or track suit on for a while, as dancers do, to keep the muscles warm and relaxed, otherwise injuries will occur — they are not just meant to be fashionable here. The warm-up should take about ten or fifteen minutes. The major joints of your body are cushioned from each other by cartilage. As you limber up the cartilages thicken by absorbing liquid, then they fit better between the bones, giving a better joint.

At the end of the session, the cooling down part should be done gradually, not hurriedly, and a bit of yoga here is helpful. Lie down on the floor and gradually, over a period of several minutes, lift your legs up to your chest, then above your head, holding each position for about thirty seconds or so. Finally stretch your legs as far over the top of your head as you can go, trying to aim for lowering them so that your knees rest on either side of your head. Then work back through the routine and lie flat on your back for about a minute. It helps if gentle music is played during this last routine. Get up gently on your right hand side, to put less strain on the heart. Then — and this goes for all exercises — put on a track suit or something equally warm and comfortable so that you don't stiffen up immediately. If you skip the cooling down part of an aerobic exercise session, the blood tends to 'pool' in the extremities of the body. As the muscles stop pumping away, the lack of oxygen-bearing blood in the brain makes the heart pump even harder than it has been forced to do in the aerobics session. You may faint as a result of all this, so gradually work down to a rest, then you won't strain your heart.

Aerobic exercises were made popular by an American doctor, Dr Kenneth Cooper, who devised them for the

United States Air Force. He believes that aerobic sports can actually slow down the ageing process. In his Aerobics Institute, in Dallas, Texas, studies have shown that people who take regular, sensible aerobic exercise generally have lower blood-pressure, and lower levels of fat in the blood-stream, lower amounts of body fat and fewer heart-beat irregularities than most other people. In some cases of hypertension, aerobic sports and exercises have actually been helpful in lowering blood-pressure — but people need to be careful if they come into this category, and seek professional guidance. Dr Cooper has always promoted this type of sport as a way of life, not just as something to be undertaken for a few minutes a week. In his view the benefit of aerobics against ageing is that when cells are deprived of oxygen they die, but because aerobic exercise feeds every part of the body, the cells of the body live on and thrive. Thousands of Americans have been witnesses to Dr Cooper's theories, and the country has seen a dramatic decrease in coronaries in recent years. There are 27 million runners in the USA — and of course there has been a great upsurge in this sport in Britain over the past few years, as for example, the success of the London Marathon has shown. Diet and the anti-smoking campaign has played a major part in decreasing the amount of heart attacks in America (unlike in this country, which has one of the highest records of heart disease in the world), but aerobic sport has also been given its due accolade as being partly responsible for this achievement.

The reason for the sharp decrease in heart attacks as a result of aerobic exercise is that unlike isometric activity which involves static muscle contraction, aerobic exercise doesn't boost blood-pressure and thereby put a strain on the heart. Aerobic sport raises the pulse from its normal rate when at rest (for men 70-85 beats a minute as usual, with 75-90 for women) to well over 100 beats a minute. The major body muscles have to work harder and blood is forced into them with such pressure that new roads of supply, new capillaries, are opened up. The veins and arteries are made more elastic and free from blockages. If a blockage does occur, the trained person can still get enough oxygen through by-passing the blockage along the collateral blood vessels. All this means is that it is important to warm up and work gradually up through these activities, in whichever sport you choose. More strain will be put on the heart if you don't.

With exercise, your breathing should improve, as the chest and abdomen muscles wake up after their usual shallow breathing and oxygen reaches a greater area of the lungs than is usual. The lungs will be better able to process oxygen and to clear out the waste toxins like carbon dioxide which poison the body. As stores of body fat are attacked by increased exercise, you will find strength to endure more activity, and to become fitter. If you jog or cycle, your legs will get the biggest benefit, although the back and waist will also be helped and firmed. Arm muscles are strengthened by running, skipping and swimming — and here there is the added benefit for women in that the pectoral muscles are strengthened and firm, giving better support and shape to the bust.

# 5

# Health and Beauty

The old adage 'beauty comes from within' is absolutely true. The best aids to beauty — and good looks in a man — are a good, balanced diet, plenty of fresh air, exercise and rest. Your face and your body are the external part — what's more important is what you put inside your body in terms of nutrients.

We don't have to be blessed with fantastic coloured eyes or thick lustrous hair, sculptured bone structure or long elegant legs, to be thought beautiful. All these attributes of course help anyone to be beautiful, but people are more impressed by personality, vitality and a look of healthiness — and that's something we can all attain. Women of thirty to fifty often look much more attractive than they did in their teens or twenties as they have learned to make the most of themselves. Obviously if you are not born a natural beauty then it is much more hard work. But healthy people exude their own type of beauty which draws others to them, whereas the person who has good features or a tall shapely body but neglects their diet and sleep will be lacking in an overall vivacity.

Apart from your balanced diet (see Chapter 2), exercise and plenty of deep, restful sleep, what can you do to improve your general appearance? Throughout history people have experimented with plants, flowers and even foods to produce beauty aids — just think of Cleopatra bathing in all that milk! During the past few years, many of the old natural remedies have regained popularity. With the help of scientists we have been able to get rid of the old myths, charming as they are in folk lore, and see what products were really beneficial. Alongside this, there has been the growth of feeling that animals should not be used in laboratory experiments, especially for cosmetics, and so the interest in using plants has risen once more.

As you get older it is good to know that you can use natural preparations on your skin and hair, made from harmless basic materials. Many natural products are available in shops, on beauty counters, in health food stores and even in chemists' shops. Be careful to read the labels to see that you are really getting natural ingredients, made with herbs or natural oils extracted from plants. Ask, if you are not sure, and if you are not satisfied that the assistant knows much about the product, try and find out about it elsewhere. Many beauty preparations, bath oils or skin creams, can be made at home from simple ingredients. If you do try this — and it is very satisfying to produce your own natural toilet or cosmetic products — use only natural containers such as glass, pottery, ceramic or enamel, never plastic. Stir them with wooden, not metal spoons, and if you can get it, use a pestle and mortar for grinding grains. You may have to keep the oil or cream in the fridge, especially if it is perishable.

The history of cosmetics is a fascinating one. The Chinese used them as far back as four thousand years ago, but probably just for medicinal use, as they were keen herbalists. The

# HEALTH AND BEAUTY

Egyptians used cosmetics to paint and colour their faces, with henna, milk, and kohl for their eyes. They also used fragrant oils for bathing. The idea of the mud pack probably originated with them. The Romans were fond of bathing preparations but they did not use cosmetics. Although the Church frowned upon cosmetics and any worldly show of vanity, during the Middle Ages the Crusaders did bring back the ideas of making fragrances and using certain oils from the East.

By the time of Elizabeth I herbalism was fully developed and most houses — especially in the countryside — had an extensive herbal garden in full use. Many herbals were written, books such as that produced by the most famous English herbalist, Nicholas Culpeper. For much of their knowledge the European herbalists relied on the ancient Greek and Roman documents. In Tudor times and up until the eighteenth century, beauty aids were more often used to cover up blemishes and disfigurements on the skin rather than enhance the eyes or add colour to areas of the face. But as hygiene improved, a wider range of beauty preparations appeared and not only the females but also the foppish dandies of the Regency era took to wearing rouge, powder and of course, the beauty spot, to add a bit of intrigue. In the nineteenth century women became delicately pretty, men more sombre, and so cosmetics were on the wane. But girls were taught how to make their own beauty preparations: scents from flowers such as violets and lavender, skin fresheners from rose-water, flowers and cucumber. Many of these are still produced today and can be found in herbal shops and on beauty counters, now scientifically tested to ensure that they do really work and that the product is of a high quality.

It is fun and gives a sense of achievement to make your

own beauty products. Many of the ingredients you will find in your kitchen or in your garden, especially in the summer and if you grow a few herbs. Otherwise you can easily buy the rest in the chemist's shop, or a herbal shop. You must first decide on your skin and hair type. Many of us have a skin that is a combination of oily and dry, and our hair type can alter slightly with the climate and our lifestyle. Central heating produces a dry heat which, coupled with less sunshine in winter, can make the hair out of condition and the skin too dry. You need to decide on your particular needs before you start buying or making any new beauty preparations.

There are many simple cleansers for which you need go no further than your kitchen. A potato cut in half and gently rubbed on the skin will cleanse it naturally; some natural yogurt is excellent for the skin, as is warm (not hot) milk. If you have a juicer then you can use potato or strawberry juice to cleanse your skin but make sure that it is fresh. A daily drink of fresh fruit or vegetable juice is a marvellous beauty aid. Vegetable oils such as almond oil or coconut oil, on a wad of cotton wool, will remove eye make-up — even mascara. Ease gently around the delicate skin tissue surrounding the eyes. Dragging a hard tissue or rubbing into the eye area will only cause damage to the eyes and make them age that much more quickly.

These cleansing creams are a little more difficult to make properly, but can be made successfully at home if you have the time and don't rush. Understanding what goes into simple natural products like these is helpful and interesting, even if you don't want to make them yourself.

## Light Cleanser

½ oz (15g) white wax
6 tablespoons almond oil
¼ teaspoon boric acid powder
5 tablespoons distilled water

1. Melt the wax in a glass bowl placed on top of a pan of simmering water — or use a double boiler if you have one. Slowly add the almond oil.
2. Warm the distilled water through then dissolve the boric acid powder in it in a dish.
3. Add this mixture to the wax and oil.
4. Remove from the heat and whisk until it thickens and becomes a cream.

## Almond Cleansing Cream

½ oz (15g) white wax
2 tablespoons hydrous lanolin
8 tablespoons almond oil
2 tablespoons rose-water

1. Melt the wax and lanolin in a double boiler or in a glass bowl over a pan of simmering water.
2. Beat it slowly and add the almond oil gradually. Then blend in the rose-water.

For another extremely effective cleanser, just take a tablespoon of fresh natural yogurt and a teaspoon of lemon juice, mix them together and apply to the face. Make this fresh each time you want to use it. After thorough cleansing, the skin needs to be freshened with a toner, or an astringent for more oily skins. Toners are lighter than astringents, which often have a base of witch-hazel, a herb grown in many gardens. Rose-water and witch-hazel extract can be bought from a pharmacist. The reason for using these liquids, soaked in cotton wool and wiped around the face, is to help close the pores after cleansing, and to stimulate the circulation. They also refine the texture of the skin and restore the acid, or pH factor, to the skin.

Again your kitchen will reveal many simple skin fresheners that your great-grandmother would have probably used — a slice of raw potato, a slice of lemon or a combination of lemon juice and water. The juice of two cucumbers, heated to boiling, with the froth skimmed off, and the liquid bottled, is a good freshener. Even a glass of a light white wine will be effective. Other old country recipes used an infusion of marigold heads (make it in a pot, like tea) or the heavenly scented elderflowers — surely one of the most evocative scents of summer.

A simple astrigent is made from two parts rose-water and one part witch-hazel. A stronger version is made from two parts witch-hazel and three parts rose-water, shaken together in a bottle — the slightly increased amount of witch-hazel making it more astringent and so more suitable for an oily skin. Some other herbs, such as sage or comfrey can be made into an infusion and added to other ingredients such as a little boric acid powder, witch-hazel, a small amount of alcohol, and some glycerine. When these mixtures are used, the astringent should be allowed to stand for at least a week before straining and using. Many herbs, such as parsley, fennel, camomile or yarrow, can be easily made into a skin freshener by simmering a handful of the leaves in a cupful of water and leaving the infusion to stand for a couple of hours.

The third stage of cleansing, and extremely important for people over thirty five or so, is the application of a moisturizer.

This gives protection to the skin in a film that clings to the skin surface and help to keep it smooth and supple. As people get older their skin tends to become drier and if it is naturally dry anyway, can age more quickly with lines and wrinkles. Simple home-made moisturizers are made from any vegetable oil, applied in a thin coating. Smooth over with a wet hand and gently blot dry. Alternatively use cucumber juice in the same way. Rose-water can be made into a moisturizing lotion, by pouring three tablespoons into a bottle and adding five tablespoons of glycerine. Shake the bottle well each time it is used. Almonds, freshly ground, can also be used. Blanch the almonds if they still have their skins on and grind with a pestle and mortar. Only one ounce should be used, and to this powder add ½ pint (285ml) of distilled water, one drop at a time. When the liquid looks milky, strain it and bottle.

Conditioning cream should be used daily on the skin as one gets older, to prevent it ageing prematurely. These creams nourish and lubricate the skin, preventing wrinkles. They can be left on for a few hours each day or overnight. Massage it with the fingertips in gentle upward movements over the face, jaw and throat, going very delicately around the eyes. Conditioners should be thoroughly cleansed off the skin afterwards. Honey and cream are excellent conditioners. After moistening the face, massage the honey into the skin and leave for twenty minutes, then rinse well. Or try a teaspoon of honey mixed with a couple of tablespoons of light cream, left on the face and throat for the same time, then rinsed off.

As one gets older, the skin becomes less firm and increasingly flabby. Many people find that when they go on a diet, especially a crash one, that their face shows it first, and the jowls look decidedly pouchy. Oil-based preparations are a great help. Firming lotions, tightening masks, firming masks, all are variations on the same theme of helping one's skin to look youthful. A tightening mask can be quickly made from an egg white, half a teaspoon of honey and one tablespoon of powdered milk. Beat them together until they are thoroughly blended, apply to the face and leave for twenty minutes, before rinsing off. This has an effect for a few hours, so would be a good idea to apply as a boost before an evening out. You'll feel all the more refreshed and revitalized if you relax for those twenty minutes with your eyes closed. Another recipe is for the throat and neck, again using an egg white. Take a teaspoon of honey, a dessertspoon of milk and the egg white, and add to all these a teaspoon of spirit of camphor, which you can buy from a chemist's shop. Mix together and apply to the throat. Leave the mask until it is completely dry then rinse off and use a good moisturizer afterwards.

You cannot take away those wrinkles and lines but they can be softened for a while to make your face look youthful again. Don't worry that you have them — laughter lines are attractive, and mature faces can have their own sense of mystery that the bland face of youth cannot possess. The best way to stop wrinkles forming on the forehead is not to frown too much and the best way to stop them appearing round the mouth is to keep your face mobile and not set it into a rigid, downward gloomy look. Adequate sleep, rest and a good diet will help tremendously. Make your own wrinkle lotion from an infusion of herbs, especially lemon balm or camomile. If you beat an egg white with a few drops of lemon juice and leave on the face until it is absolutely dry, you will help soften the lines. There are several anti-wrinkle creams on the market, but they tend to be very expensive. Look for the more natural ones in the skin care ranges available at health food stores and herbal shops.

Facial exercises often help to keep the face looking mobile.

## HEALTH AND BEAUTY

Use a mirror, pretend that you are screaming at someone. Open your mouth into a wide circle, so that your jaw bone feels tight. Relax — and you'll feel less tense. Then fill your cheeks with air, purse the lips and blow out slowly. This exercise is also good for asthma and bronchitis sufferers.

Men often do the following exercise without realizing it, when they are shaving. Purse the lips a little and then push your mouth towards the right ear, then the left one. Lastly, brace the muscles at the front of the throat by pushing the chin down strongly and pulling back the sides of the mouth. Try these exercises often (particularly if you are alone!) to avoid getting an old, 'set' look on your face.

Aching, tired eyes cannot look beautiful. Frequent blinking, and looking downwards often helps. Try the relaxation exercises in Chapter 4. Move the eyes up, down and from side to side, and try screwing them up tightly, then opening them wide. The most soothing thing you can do for tired eyes is to cut a couple of thick slices of cucumber, then lie down with the slices covering each eye. It is the most marvellous tonic if you give yourself enough time — and if you wear eye make-up you'll need time to re-apply it.

Many women still, at over thirty five, have skin that is rather oily and prone to acne or blackheads. Diet can help, but there are special preparations that can help dry the skin and reduce blemishes without losing the basic good oils which prevent wrinkling and actually help these people to look younger for longer. Oily skin must be kept absolutely clean or there will be infections in the pores which tend to get clogged. Oatmeal and lemon juice is a good cleanser, as grains rubbed into the skin are very good for dislodging the oil in the pores. Use a mild allergy-free soap, then an astringent, as outlined before. Conditioners are not needed — unless you have been over fastidious and have made some areas, such as the cheeks, rather dry. Remember that most of us have a combination skin. Use a facial once a week — don't use the types with honey or egg yolk. Brewer's yeast and yogurt mixed together are good, and so is cucumber, a little powdered milk and an egg white. A light wine, just a cupful, with the juice of a lemon added, is a good remedy for blackheads, or a cup of ground almonds and some water, rubbed into the pores. There are many grain-based products on the market which are suitable.

## Hands

Hands need special protection as you get older, especially in our climate. We need extra lubrication in the skin anyway during the winter, with drying winds outside and equally dry central heating indoors. Thick rubber gloves should be worn when washing up or doing any work that involves using water. It is also a good idea to wear cotton gloves when doing the housework, and with a protective barrier cream smoothed over the hands before putting them on. Always wear gloves when gardening and if you can, when painting or decorating the house — just an old pair of gloves will be fine, as they will fit your hands well, better than clumsy rubber gloves.

In the summer we forget to protect our hands because they don't get so dry and chapped as in the winter months. But it is still necessary to work cream into the hands each day, after washing your hands and before going to bed. Sun and wind can be extremely drying, and even more so if they are combined with the salty atmosphere of the seaside. Some cucumber juice mixed with an equal amount of witch-hazel will ease chapped hands, as will soaking the hands in a bowl of milk (cold or just warm) nightly for five minutes. If you have dirtied your hands and the stain is particularly stubborn, wipe your hands with a slice of lemon, and the stain should come away. A mild solution of cider vinegar and water, used as a rinse after washing, helps keep the hands soft and less likely to become chapped. Cider vinegar is also good for strengthening the nails — dip the fingernails into cider vinegar for five minutes each night.

Try to give yourself a weekly manicure — perhaps as you wait for your face-pack to dry. Soften and lubricate the cuticles with either a proprietary brand of cuticle softener, available in many cosmetic ranges, or with a mixture of pineapple juice, egg yolk (a couple of tablespoons of each) and just half a teaspoon of cider vinegar. Soak the nails in the mixture for 30 minutes. For the bought cuticle softeners follow the instructions on the bottle. Another mixture to strengthen nails is made from equal parts of castor oil and glycerine, rubbed into the fingertips and cuticles. Remember to rinse these mixtures away thoroughly afterwards, and then always use a good hand cream. A good diet with plenty of minerals, fresh fruit and vegetables, will help your hands and nails to be healthy and strong.

Keep your hands supple by tightening and then releasing them quite often. Work the fingers as if you are playing the piano — in itself a good exercise for the hands and the mind, too, if you can manage it. Sit with your wrists resting on a support — your thighs, the steering wheel of a car or the arms of a chair. Stretch the fingers and thumbs up and out, making as much space as possible between them. Then let them go, so that they fall back on to their support. This is good for people who tend to clench their fists — and would be an excellent exercise to do in a traffic jam, instead of heightening your feeling of tension by fuming at the cars in front of you.

For hands and fingers to be mobile, your wrists must be equally so. With your arms held straight out in front of you, and elbows locked, lift your hands up and back as far as possible, fingers stretching upwards. Push the hands down, so that the fingers point to the floor. Another exercise to make your wrists more flexible, is to hold the arms out in front with the elbows locked again and not able to bend. Then make circles in the air with your hands, keeping your arms absolutely straight. Rotate one way, then the other. Actually, if your arms are lifted up to shoulder level and pointed out at each side of you and the wrists are rotated in this way, you'll be not only making your wrists more mobile but firming the chest or bust as well.

Massage your hands — much more so than when you apply hand cream. Hold one hand at a time with the other hand, then apply a series of thumb frictions to the wrist, especially to any areas around the tendons that feel tight. Work over the palm in the same way, releasing any frictions you may feel. Place the length of your right thumb along the base of the palm of the left hand, letting your fingers cradle the back of the hand. Starting at the outer edge of the hand, make deep strokes with your thumb from wrist to fingertips. With each stroke move your thumb further in towards the index finger. Then turn the hand over and, supporting the palm, make more thumb frictions to the back of the wrist and from wrist to fingers, working between the bones. This last massage exercise should really be done by another person, holding your hands in theirs, and taking hold of the base of a finger between the thumb and fingers. Get your partner to pull firmly and slowly up the length of the finger, continuing a little way beyond the fingertips. Before reaching the end of the first finger, they should begin pulling the next one with your hand and repeat this with all the fingers and thumbs, releasing only one at a time so that the hand is always supported.

## Feet

The American nutritionist Gayelord Hauser once remarked, 'Aching feet make wrinkles'. He went on to denounce most of us for neglecting our feet, punishing them day after day with no reward, pinching them into unsuitable footwear and generally ignoring them. We are so hard on our feet that we take for granted their dry, hardened appearance and even the corns and blisters. If you do suffer from foot problems, consult a chiropodist and keep to regular treatments. Otherwise, ease up on your feet. Wear shoes that support your feet and legs, not teetering high heels and pointed toes that throw the weight on to the ball of the foot and shorten the calf muscles. Go barefoot as often as you can and encourage your children to do so — they will thank you when they are your age. Any heel that is over an inch high is damaging to the feet, so limit wearing high heeled shoes. Go to a reputable shoe shop that will measure your feet, and never wear plastic shoes. Only leather can allow the feet to breathe and you'll be storing up all sorts of trouble for yourself if you wear plastic or other man-made materials, however much they resemble leather.

Feet that are killing you are doing precisely that. You will age fast with poor footwear. Make sure that your diet includes plenty of calcium found in milk and cheese, for good bones, vitamin C in citrus fruits, and vitamin D. Get plenty of air and sun to your feet and walk briskly in flat walking shoes whenever you can. After bathing, massage your feet (and legs, for they will probably be suffering with dry skin as well) with a good moisturizing cream. Use good quality talcum or foot powder between the toes so that the skin does not flake and so that damp conditions do not foster fungal conditions between the toes.

A hot foot-bath containing two tablespoons of bicarbonate

of soda helps to soften callouses and corns. After drying, rub in a mixture of a little oil and a couple of teaspoons of vinegar. Bathe tired feet in lukewarm water with some Epsom salts thrown into it. The old mustard baths used to warm up cold or wet feet are still a good idea. Just add a pinch of mustard powder to the hot water and soak for ten minutes. A few drops of lavender oil in a foot-bath or in an ordinary bath will revive tired feet. Natural yogurt softens the feet — add a teaspoon of malt vinegar to a carton of natural yogurt (or a cup of home-made) and smear this all over the feet and between the toes. Leave it on for five minutes before rinsing off.

Massaging the feet is best done by another person, but you can do a certain amount on your own. Supporting the feet on the floor or bed, make deep strokes with both hands along the length of the foot to the ends of the toes. Repeat this five times. Then, supporting the foot with both hands make thumb frictions round the inner and outer ankle bones and to the top of the foot, working from ankle to toes between the bones. Then place both thumbs on top of the foot, near the middle of the toes, letting the fingers curl round to the sole of the foot. With each stroke, move a little further towards the ankle. The next exercise works on the sole. Give frictions with the thumb from the heel to the toes and from the outer to the inner edges of the foot. Then stroke deeply up the sole from heel to toes, supporting the foot all the time. Make the base of your palm cover the width of the foot. Repeat this twice over. Lastly, firmly and slowly, pull each toe between the thumb and forefinger, working through all the toes, and then go through all the exercises for the other foot.

Swollen ankles are usually caused by fluid retention, and diet and rest will cure this. The foods that will help are fresh fruits, and vegetables such as asparagus, celery, cucumber,

# HEALTH AND BEAUTY

artichokes, pumpkin, marrow and courgettes. Even parsley, horseradish, nettle (cooks and tastes like spinach) and dandelion are useful. The latter can be bought as a tea in health food stores. Juicers are very helpful here as the fresh juices are even more beneficial. Water retention can be caused by poor circulation and by kidney problems, among other causes, so you should consult a doctor if this is a continuing problem. Avoid salt in your diet altogether. Aerobic exercise, to music, or the sports mentioned in Chapter 4, will help reduce fluid retention. Relaxing with your feet supported higher than your head, for fifteen minutes a day, will ease tired aching feet and puffy ankles. They should feel rather tingly afterwards.

One of the very best exercises for tired flat feet is to move around on your toes. Try it to music and aim to walk on your toes for five minutes. Work up to this by doing a little each day if you find it too much of a strain. Afterwards put your feet in the shower or the bath and let warm water run over them, then cold. Let the water run over them for a minute or two at a time before switching taps. Your feet will feel years younger after this treat.

## Teeth

Thankfully fewer people over forty need to wear dentures these days. With good dental hygiene and a balanced diet containing plenty of nutrients people should be able to keep their teeth all their lives. Regular check-ups are necessary, every six months or so. So are trips to the dental hygienist, which your dentist will arrange for you. The hygienist scales and polishes the teeth, making them altogether more attractive than before — and you feel rather guilty eating anything afterwards, especially of the cake and biscuit variety! Orthodontic treatment is also available for adults as well as children, to correct irregular teeth. This does tend to be rather expensive and may not be worth it for some people although in America it seems almost to be the fashion as so many middle-aged people are to be seen wearing teeth braces.

Good strong teeth need plenty of calcium, found in milk and cheese, and vitamins A, C and D, as well as phosphorus, found in fresh fruit and vegetables. Teeth need to be kept working right through your life — soft, mushy foods that need hardly any chewing will not exercise them at all. Of course sugar and any type of sweets will decay them very quickly, especially as you get older. Do without these in your diet, or at least keep them to the very minimum, and that goes for any sweet drink, such as cola.

Bleeding gums are one of the first signs of a deficiency of vitamin C which is found in tomatoes, citrus fruits and green peppers. Take fish-liver oil capsules for your vitamin D intake each day. Get enough sunshine when you can, which is not always easy in our climate, hence the need for this vitamin supplement. Vitamin D is essential for the full utilization of calcium in the body.

Fresh rhubarb juice, taken with honey and fresh strawberry juice is a beauty tonic not only for the teeth but the whole body and is often used on health farms. A good diet and regular, careful brushing (check with your dentist that you are still doing it the correct way) should give you good teeth forever. If however, you do have to wear dentures or partial dentures, it is not the end of the world. So many improvements have been made in this field, and dentures are not the ageing things they used to be. They fit so much better and can even sometimes improve on nature. But again, a good diet is necessary to stop the gums from shrinking too far and to hold the dentures firmly in place. Take plenty of calcium and phosphorous each day remembering it is as important now as when you had a full set of natural teeth.

Pyorrhoea is another name for gum disease, where the jaw bones become so destroyed by poor diet that the teeth can no longer be kept in place. The gums can be actually seen to recede, showing more tooth root, eventually causing tooth decay. This is particularly a problem for middle-aged people in the Western world, due to an over-refined, soft, rich diet. Studies by doctors like Sir Robert McCarrison and Dr Weston A. Price in the USA, have shown that people elsewhere in the world who do not live on a rich diet refined of all its natural goodness, have no problems with this disease. In other experiments, animals were given just below adequate amounts of vitamin C. A similar condition to pyorrhoea was found in these animals. However, all vitamins, and calcium and phosphorus are necessary — and must be taken daily — to prevent this disease. Even if pyorrhoea is already under way, it can be treated and the disease will recede if a balanced vitamin and mineral rich diet is adopted.

Fresh strawberry juice rubbed on the teeth helps keep them clean — as will sage leaves. Or dip your toothbrush in some apple juice and clean the teeth. Apple cider vinegar has so many beauty uses — this time add a teaspoon to a little water and clean your teeth after a meal to remove the plaque that forms on the enamel. You can make your own refreshing mouthwash from one teaspoon of bicarbonate of soda and one of salt in a glass of water, or from an infusion of one part mint to two parts water.

## Hair

Immaculate looking, clean hair that has gloss and bounce, cut into an easy-to-maintain, attractive style, must be one of the best ways to keep looking youthful. A good diet and adequate rest is again as essential for your hair as for other parts of the body — you are what you eat, after all. It needs feeding from the inside with plenty of vitamins, especially of the B group, and the minerals iron, iodine and copper. A lack of iodine can make your hair a problem. Anyone with a hair problem should take supplements of those 'wonder foods', brewer's yeast and wheatgerm. For more about these, see Chapter 3. Eat as many fresh fruits and vegetables as you can and drink fresh juices. Get enough sleep, fresh air and exercise.

The B vitamins are thought to be helpful in keeping the grey at bay — even to restoring hair colour. But don't expect to swallow some B vitamin supplements and sit back to await a miracle. You need to eat more like the Chinese, said Gayelord Hauser, who took his knowledge from anthropologists' studies. They eat foods that are rich in the B vitamins, unpolished wholegrain rice, fish, soya beans, root vegetables and herbs, and they cook their vegetables for the minimum amount of time, making the most of the vitamins and minerals present in the foods. The Bulgarians, whose national dish is yogurt, rich in B vitamins, have very little grey hair. So have the Irish, who eat a lot of iodine in their sea food, in their water and in sea 'greens' such as carrageen moss (which is found in health food stores, particularly in delicious vegetarian jelly crystals). Drinking great amounts of coffee — bad for you anyway — may be causing grey hair in many people. Studies in America have shown that consuming large quantities of coffee may have this effect. Other effects of vitamin B deficiencies were found in laboratory-tested animals, including grey hair, and so it may be that coffee attacks B vitamins in the body. For good health, try drinking less coffee, or drink the decaffeinated type instead, and you may find that your hair stays its own colour. Of course it could be that grey hair, or thinning hair, is hereditary in your family but these efforts may help to minimize the end result.

After feeding your hair from the inside, you need to feed it on the outside too. After using a good shampoo, suitable for your hair type, condition your hair. It is not always necessary to use a conditioner at every shampooing, unless your hair is noticeably out of condition. Some experts say once a week, others once a month — you will know when your hair needs it. If you bleach, tint or colour your hair, or if you have it permed, the chemicals put on to the hair will make it necessary for frequent conditioning. This is especially the case with dry hair, with the effect of so many chemicals added to the already dry state of the hair. Heated rollers, using very hot hairdryers close to the head, curling tongs and hot brushes — all these electrical aids, however useful, will take their toll on your hair, drying it out. Central heating will have the same effect.

Shampoos and conditioners using natural ingredients are best for your hair as you get older. There are many good herbal lines available, especially in beauty shops and in health food stores. Try to do without clogging hair sprays. There are several new types of setting gel and styling mousse on the market now. Don't use them to excess.

If you have a problem scalp, rosemary, thyme or nettle shampoos will be best for you. Work the shampoo into the scalp and leave it on for a few minutes, before rinsing well in warm, not hot water. Shampoo again if necessary.

Brush the hair vigorously, with a good stiff hairbrush that stimulates the scalp. This will get the circulation going in that area and you will certainly see the difference in your shining head of hair. Give your scalp a good massage every day. Don't wear a tight hat or scarf, stopping the air circulating round your head. Let it blow in the wind or the sun. Even the rain, especially fine misty rain, will do it good.

Let your hair be natural — not full of artificial chemicals. As you get older and some grey does creep into your hair, have it lightened if the sight of the grey depresses you. There's nothing like a change of style or colour to give a woman a lift — don't feel guilty about it! Put good natural ingredients into your diet and make sure the other hair preparations you use are natural ones.

Camomile is good for fair hair; beer or vinegar for dark hair types. Sage, rosemary and egg shampoos are also good for dark hair — you can make your own from an infusion of the herbs in a cup, with an egg yolk beaten into it for dry hair, or an egg white for oily hair. Olive oil is good for dry hair, especially if the ends are very damaged. You should warm a couple of tablespoons of the oil and gently massage into the scalp. Comb it through, then wrap the head in a steaming towel. Leave it like this for up to half an hour, reheating the towel if you want. Then shampoo off and rinse well. Avocado, mashed and massaged into the hair and scalp, covered with foil or plastic for an hour before shampooing, is good for all types of hair.

Hair conditioners can be easily made, at a fraction of the cost of the bought ones. Mix together a teaspoon of honey with two teaspoons of sesame or safflower oil in a bowl over a pan of simmering water. Beat an egg into the mixture and stir slowly until it is thoroughly even, before using.

Make a warm oil conditioner in this way. Pick or buy some herbs — any type of your choice or from what is available, such as camomile, sage, rosemary or southernwood for instance — and lightly bruise them with a rolling pin. Loosely fill a glass jar. Cover the herbs with oil and tie perforated paper or muslin over the mouth of the jar and place it on a warm — not too hot — sunny window sill. It could also

## HEALTH AND BEAUTY

be put near a warm stove. Shake or stir the herbs every day and make sure they don't get too hot or the contents will turn musty and begin to cook. In two weeks or so the herbs will have given their rich oils to the milder oil in the jar. Strain the jar, pressing the herbs to get all their oils out. When you want to use the herbal oil as a conditioner, warm it through and then rub well into the hair and scalp. Cover the hair with a plastic bag or shower cap and wrap it tightly in a warm towel and leave for at least 15 minutes. Warm up the towel again if necessary.

There are many herbs which will do your hair so much good in shampoos, conditioners and just as a final rinse. Rosemary and sage will darken the hair, and are excellent tonics and conditioners. Stinging nettle, southernwood, goosegrass and burdock help against dandruff, while catmint soothes scalp irritations. Witch-hazel leaves are astringent and cleansing, as are soapwort. Nasturtium helps hair to grow, while parsley enriches colour and gives lustre. Marigold and mullein flowers will lighten the hair colour. Enquire at a herbal shop and experiment with preparations made from these delightful plants or better still, grow your own herbs and make your preparations yourself, it is an absorbing, restful hobby.

Henna is a natural hair colouring that will not harm your hair and the effect will last for several months. But be warned — while it is not toxic, it is very astringent, so try a patch test first on your head to see if you suit it. Also, if it is not used properly, the shades of henna can be dramatic to say the least — and a very hard colour for an older woman. It is best done by a professional but if you feel capable of achieving the right result and an attractive shade, shampoo the hair well and wear a pair of rubber gloves. If you mix herbs into the henna powder mix, such as sage to make it more auburn than red, or camomile to bring reddish tones to brunettes, you can vary the shade. Camomile, made into a bleaching paste, can be used to lighten the hair. An infusion of sage leaves and strong tea, steeped for a long time and dabbed on to the hair is supposed to bring back the brown to grey hair. Whatever colour you choose or whether you do it yourself with shop or home-made preparations, make sure it is not too harsh. Very blonde or very black, even very auburn hair, looks hard and that is in itself ageing. There are many softer shades available nowadays — grey hair does not even have to be 'transformed' with the blue rinse favoured by dowager-type ladies.

Have your hair cut well in a soft flattering style and go back to the hairdressers every four to six weeks to keep it in shape. Men look better as they get older in a hair-style that is not too severe and short — but again extremes do not flatter. The sight of older men with quite long hair, and probably thinning balding pates on top is not a pretty sight. It should be styled fairly short and neat.

## Sunbathing

Many people have been sun worshippers for years — and the result is, in hot countries, that they have skin like wrinkled walnuts. We know now that while sunshine is of great benefit and provides the body with vitamin D, too much can dry the skin excessively and even cause skin cancer. There probably isn't much chance of getting skin cancer from too much direct sun in this country, but many of us know of the bad and painful effects of overdoing suntanning.

Peeling, dried skin is unsightly. Use a good sun-tan oil, made from natural oils and apply it again if you have been swimming — unless it is of the type that withstands water. Use a lip balm to prevent dry, blistering lips. Gradually get your skin accustomed to a little more sun each day when it is hot or you are on holiday. Remember you can catch too much sun even if you are gardening or painting outside windows, for instance — that's just the time when you are likely to forget that you are suntanning while you are working. So don't forget to apply a good sun-tan cream when you are doing outside work if it is hot. Remember also to cover your head with a shady hat or at least a scarf if you are going to be in hot, direct sun for a long time. If the sun does not suit you, if it gives you a headache or a rash even with creams, then take only ten minutes or so in the sun. Then find a shady spot and don't worry if your skin is still pale.

If you are sunbathing, try not to do so in the heat of the day between noon and two o'clock. It's best in the early morning before eleven or after three o'clock, for anyone of any age. High in the Swiss Alps a doctor called Rollier started his sunbathing clinics for sick people and his advice is good for all of us. Never sunbathe for more than an hour a day and only expose a portion of the body at a time — the legs for the first two days, then the upper parts of the body for fifteen minutes when the legs are browned, then when they are tanned, the back gets the sun. After sunning yourself, use a good after-sun milk to moisturize the skin, and cover up with something flowing and loose. You will feel extremely relaxed and free from headaches or any other pains — if you have followed these guidelines.

## Bathing

A luxurious soak in a warm scented bath does anyone a power of good. Bathing is more than a necessity — it can be a luxury, given the time and the ingredients for it. It can also be a brisk rub-down type of bath — this gets the circulation going and is excellent for you as you get older. Wash with a good non-alkaline soap, then with a loofah or a body mitt, and briskly rub the skin all over the body in small vigorous movements. The skin will feel smoother and your circulation will be all the better for it — especially on a cold wintry day when you feel rather sluggish.

The lazy, luxury bath can be kept for the evening and especially to induce deep relaxed sleep. Baths can be draining and are not always the best thing to get you going when there is a lot to do. They are marvellous for winding down though, especially if you add some herbs or aromatic oils to the bath as it is running. These are really more beneficial than foam baths, which dissolve as soon as any soap gets into the water. There are various aromatic oils available — lavender to calm the nerves, yin yang to stimulate the senses. Herbs are a simpler method and much cheaper — tie them in a muslin bag and leave in the bath. Lie back in the warm, not too hot, water for at least fifteen minutes to get the benefit of the aroma and the natural oils of the herbs. Dandelion leaves, chamomile, lemon balm, rosemary, mint or lemon verbena — whatever you can find or buy, try them. If you haven't any muslin, tie them up in the foot of an old pair of tights. Relax in the water and try one or two ankle and leg exercises while you soak. Raise your leg up and down, then the other leg, then revolve the ankle, then the other one. Try to use your stomach muscles as you get out of the bath, rather than struggle up using the rail.

If you suffer from dry skin, add a tablespoon of olive oil to the bath. Everyone, after bathing, should moisturize their skin with a good cream, especially their legs and feet, elbows and hands. Dust the toes with a good talcum powder.

If you can, take your time and relax over your bath routine. Manicure and pedicure your nails afterwards, remove unwanted hair, apply face creams, splash with eau-de-Cologne

# HEALTH AND BEAUTY

to freshen up, especially if it is hot or muggy. Enjoy it and relax, and if you are not going to bed straight away, lie down or relax in a chair before rushing off anywhere.

Special baths available at health clubs and hotels, such as saunas, Turkish baths, or spa baths, are treats for some people. Others find that they induce headaches, especially if they cannot take too much steam or hot water as in the case of the spa baths. Spa baths are taken in the jacuzzi type tub, which is becoming popular in Britain after many years of use in America. The hot jets of water play on your body while you soak and are extremely good for tired people, for arthritis and rheumatism. Give them a try if you can. They are relaxing and also invigorating.

## Sleep

Possibly the best beauty aid of all — for any age, and for both sexes. Regular, deep sleep is needed every night. Remember all the sayings your mother ever told you about 'early to bed . . .' and 'an hour before midnight is worth two afterwards . . .'? They are all true! Calcium tablets taken with vitamin D and a glass of warm milk are better than sleeping pills if you find it hard to get to sleep. Or take a glass of lemon or orange juice and honey. Vitamin $B_6$ is another aid to sleep and for calming nerves. Practice the relaxation methods on page 72. Probably your muscles are too tense and your mind is still working through the events of the day. Try to relax your body and free your mind of all problems. Above all, do not worry about getting to sleep — that will only stop you getting to sleep at all.

# 6

# Giving Up Alcohol and Smoking

**Alcohol**
While a glass of wine is reckoned to do you good, stimulating the digestive juices at a meal, making you feel more relaxed and happy, strong alcohol will not help you to keep and look younger, especially if taken in large amounts regularly. The fact that you don't reel over, and you don't perhaps feel drunk at all, is no guide to what alcohol is actually doing to your body. The body gets used to high levels of alcohol, taken over a period of time, and your blood alcohol levels may be quite high. Women have a lower level of fluid in their body, and so absorb alcohol more quickly than men of the same weight. Their blood alcohol levels will also be higher.

Some lifestyles are more associated with problems of alcohol. Over the past few years there has been an increase in alcoholism, particularly among women, who can now easily buy drink at their supermarket along with their other shopping. Too much alcohol causes poor work performance, accidents, family quarrels, child neglect, loss of friends, marriage break-ups, even a loss of one's home and settled life. It can lead to physical and mental health breakdowns, many diseases from gastritis and peptic ulcers to cirrhosis of the liver, from brain disorders to depression and even suicide. People who take drugs, even prescribed ones, with alcohol, are seriously at risk of further ill health or death. Then, of course, drunken driving leads to trouble with the police, possibly the loss of one's licence, and maybe even the death of the driver or passenger or innocent pedestrian.

Sometimes you can drink increasing amounts over a period of time without realizing it. If you drink at least fifteen or more drinks each day then you are heavily at risk of contracting liver disease and the other associated problems of alcoholism. One of the main problems, alcoholics always say, is to admit that you are one. It is a disease, and if it affects you — you need help. You can't give it up on your own. Many people would get a shock if they totted up the number of drinks they had taken in a week. Try to aim for no more than twenty four drinks a week — and spread them out, some days not drinking at all. Try not to drink more than three pints of lager or beer a day or the equivalent in wine and not for more than half the week. Try to cut down gradually, each week. Look at the problems that might make you drink more and see if they can be helped at all. If worries such as job or money troubles, are sorted out or at least brought more out in the open by discussion (and not with the barmaid) then the drinking will probably diminish.

Try not to drink hard spirits, or limit them severely, for they cause the most damage to your system. You may have to avoid some occasions or places that involve heavy drinking, or leave early or go later to limit the amount you'll drink. Learn to give an excuse if an eager host tries to offer you more drink — saying that you are driving is the easiest one, or that you are on a diet, or have had some stomach trouble. If you are entertaining, remember that some people want to abstain and are finding it hard, so don't keep on pressing them to drink. Prepare some non-alcoholic drinks, such as the fruit juice cocktails mentioned in Chapter 3 and make them look as attractive, or more so, than alcoholic drinks. Don't keep filling up the glasses of people who don't want another, especially if you know they have got to drive later on.

Gaylord Hauser was one nutritionist who saw little harm in beer and wine, which is 'festive and cheerful', but knew that hard spirits are high in calories and can diminish interest in good food. He adds that alcohol is acid forming and creates the need for more and more vitamins, especially those of the B family.

If you can, go very easy on the hard liquor and enjoy instead a glass or two of wine or beer on a social occasion with friends, knowing that a little wine will give you some natural digestive enzymes. Too much will make you ill — and more ill than you think.

## Smoking

For whatever reasons — and psychiatrists have put forward a whole list of them — many people continue to smoke, despite all the health warnings that abound these days. Smoking is on the decline among adults (although there are signs that many youngsters are smoking early and fairly heavily) because of health and economic reasons. For many people, though, it is a habit that is hard to kick. Research studies have shown that smoking has been linked with an increased need for caffeine and sugar, and that smoking goes with alcohol — there are twice as many smokers among regular drinkers as among non-drinkers.

Heavy smoking means taking more than 20 cigarettes a day, but even moderate smokers are endangering their health, especially in the middle years. There is a strong link between smoking and lung cancer, and now also between smoking and heart disease. In the USA the drop in deaths from heart disease in the past twenty years is due in part to a 25 per cent reduction in the numbers of male smokers. Some doctors say that smoking is not the only cause of lung cancer as only one in eight of heavy smokers develops lung cancer. They argue that both heredity and diet play a part; a person's personality and the environment around him are other factors. But all these, although they may have an effect, do not take away the overall dangers to health from smoking.

When we smoke we take in toxins, like the heavy metal cadmium, which makes the lung tissue lose its elasticity and breathing becomes hard, resulting in the chronic respiratory disease, emphysema. We take in benzpyrene, another toxic substance found in tobacco tar. It covers the mucous surface of the breathing organs from the nose to the lungs. It makes the cough reflex paralysed, a reflex which would normally cause an immediate cough in response to hot smoke being breathed in. It results in the characteristic hacking and spitting of the smoker's cough which appears first thing in the morning until the first cigarette suppresses the reflex. Practically all lung cancer patients are smokers — up to 95 per cent of them — and everyone who smokes 20 or more cigarettes a day stands a chance of contracting the disease. In non-smokers the chance of getting lung cancer is one in about 220 — in smokers it is about one in eight. If you have been smoking all your life from your teens onwards, then you are more predisposed to contracting lung cancer.

If you don't get lung cancer, then it is likely that you will eventually suffer from chronic bronchitis. This affects men more than women, even if their smoking habits are the same, but the bronchial infections are similar. You are also much more likely to suffer from heart trouble in middle age if you smoke heavily — men and women alike. If you have high blood-pressure, which can lead to heart attacks, and you smoke as well, then you are doubly at risk. People with high levels of cholesterol in their blood are at risk also, so diet is another factor which must be watched if you smoke — cut out as much fat as you can from your food, and keep to polyunsaturated vegetable oils. Sometimes the flow of blood to the legs is impaired by cigarette smoke bringing toxins into the blood-stream, and this can lead to gangrene and perhaps amputation.

There has been established a link between smoking and cancer of the bladder, and of the prostate gland as well as with other cancers involving the tongue and mouth area and the throat. Smoking can cause gastro-intestinal diseases as well, started when hunger pangs are diminished by taking cigarettes, thus stopping the flow of the gastric juices and other functions in the intestine. Smoking has been discovered to interfere with the healing of ulcers, making the condition worse and more dangerous. Many more patients who smoke heavily are likely to die from ulcers than if they were non-smokers. Expectant mothers are warned to stop smoking during their pregnancy as it has been found that babies born to mothers who smoke are smaller, and there is a higher number of neo-natal deaths and still births among this group of mothers. Other diseases linked with smoking are cirrhosis of the liver, and a rare form of blindness.

If you are a non-smoker, but you live in the same house or work in the same place as a heavy smoker, then you, too, are at risk from the smoky environment. And although pipe smoking and cigar smoking are less hazardous to the individual concerned, as less toxins are inhaled, there is more danger to a person who lives or works with a heavy pipe smoker. For a non-smoker, an hour with a pipe smoker is

# GIVING UP ALCOHOL AND SMOKING

the equivalent to smoking four cigarettes themselves.

Smoking really is an anti-social habit — putting not only yourself but those around you at risk of contracting a serious disease in middle age or later. It is hard to kick the habit, but many people have found that they can. Others have cut down considerably on the number of cigarettes they smoke a day. It helps if you switch to a low tar type of cigarette — the amount of tar is stated on the packet. Rather than try to cut them out straight away, ration yourself to a progressively smaller amount each week. Don't inhale so deeply, and try not to inhale at all if you can. Use a filter, and don't smoke the cigarette to the very last inch, or less. Smoke a cigar instead, if it helps. Perhaps allow yourself a cigarette at certain times of day, and give yourself a treat for trying hard. Don't have a bag of boiled sweets or mints to eat instead of the cigarettes you crave — that will only rot your teeth, make you overweight and add to your health problems.

Many people have a craving for food when they give up or cut down on smoking. This is partly a replacement for smoking, partly due to the fact that your appetite, which has been depressed by smoking, is making a comeback. As long as you eat healthy balanced meals, without sugary snacks or sweets in between, you will feel better and healthier within a short time. Other hings to help: chew a sugar-free gum to break the habit, take fairly large doses of vitamin B complex to calm your nerves, and a supplement of vitamin C to help replace the amount you lost while you were smoking.

Some people need to go to a hypnotist to stop themselves smoking, but this does not work for everyone. There are health education departments and organizations that can give you further help. There are also anti-smoking clinics and groups — even your local doctor will help. Talk to people who have given up smoking and ask their advice.

Whatever you do, remember that by giving up smoking you will be increasing your life expectancy; you will be cutting down the risk of contracting a major illness, or will be better able to fight off any conditions such as bronchitis that you already suffer from; if you are pregnant, you will have a much better chance of having a healthy, beautiful baby; you will have more resistance to colds, coughs and many other ailments; your lungs and heart will work much more efficiently; and not least, you will feel and look good, while you and your home will lose that nasty stale smell of tobacco — and the dirt that goes with all that smoke.

# 7

# Take a Look at Your Life

All the areas of health we have looked at so far will do your body a power of good, helping to rejuvenate you and keep you that way all through your life. Hopefully it will help prolong your life as well, and in an active way, not as a sedentary person who watches the world go by. By helping your body achieve more you should also be revitalizing your mind.

The later years see many changes in our lives. Our children grow up and move away, maybe get married and we become grandparents — often while we still feel and look very youthful. People lose their jobs through company changes and redundancy and have to re-evaluate their lives. Illness, death, bereavement . . . without getting maudlin it is easy to see that we need to be fit and healthy to cope with all that. Our nerves have to be in peak condition to adapt to the changes that must inevitably happen with time.

If you eat wisely, sleep soundly, and exercise adequately, you are building a strong foundation as you get older. The main point is to adapt but not to feel older. Say 'I'm only forty-four' or whatever, instead of 'I'm nearly forty-five'. Meet the challenge by taking up new interests and meeting new people, so that you don't get stale and in a rut. This is especially important if you have to face the future after a divorce or bereavement, but also after the family have left home and the place seems rather empty instead of crowded and noisy. Then you may realize that there are compensations in the amount of time you have to take up the hobbies you always meant to have a go at but never had the time . . .

## Organic Gardening

One of the best possible hobbies you could pursue is gardening, of the organic kind. Growing your own fruit and vegetables is extremely satisfying, even more so if you know that you have used only natural methods. Organic gardening uses only the natural ways that gardeners used to employ — no artificial chemicals of any sort, no sprays, no weed-killers and no artificial fertilizers to harm the soil and the environment. The food you produce is tastier, with more flavour and colour, it is safer because no chemicals have been used, and the way you garden is much easier, because you can forget about digging.

The first rule is to get good compost. Start a compost bin in a corner of the garden with all your kitchen waste, the contents of the vacuum cleaner bag, grass mowings. Keep it activated by turning it and let it become hot. Insects and worms will do the rest for you, working it until it is well rotted and ready to spread.

Lightly mulch the earth with the compost and you will not need to dig it. The earth will become light, soft and crumbly and will not dry out under the mulches. The weeds will be smothered and you can sit back and watch everything grow naturally and lusciously. The fruits and vegetables you grow should be ten times more nutritious and flavoursome than those grown with chemical aids. You will be putting back into the soil the vitamins, minerals and other nutrients it lacked before. Chemicals destroy millions of valuable insects as well as the ones that are a pest to our crops. It is now realized that sprays can be dangerous to human beings as well as to animals, and they are being linked with cancers among some experts. Certainly, bought fruit and vegetables should be washed before eating in case they are contaminated. Commercial fertilizers may force feed plants with the major nutrients like potassium, nitrogen and phosphorus, but they leave out a whole list of other nutrients. As the plants are deficient so are the animals and humans fed on them. It is no wonder then that we have not solved all the misery of illness in the world, but in some cases have only added to it.

If you can, find a corner in your organic garden for a group of herbs. Not only will they add different flavours to your cooking and be delicious sprinkled over salads and soups, but they are aromatic on warm summer evenings, full of butterflies and bees and utterly relaxing to sit beside. Many more varieties are now available at garden centres, shops and market stalls. You'll probably be able to get a lot of cuttings and young plants from friends and find a shared interest. Plan your herb garden so that tall stately plants such as the graceful ferny fennel, strong growing lemon balm and horse-radish for instance can stand at the back, while small cushion-like plants such as camomile, chives and dwarf varieties are best at the front. Make your herb garden formal as the Elizabethans did, with little paths between the plants set out in patterns — modern paving stones are very suitable for achieving this type of effect; or have a gloriously informal herb garden, with all the plants tumbling over each other, with their contrasting leaves and flowers, their scents intermingling. Herbs can be used in so many ways: to decorate your table and put into your cool summer drinks (especially the eau-de-Cologne mint), to add to your bath water for a fragrant therapeutic soak, to make into your own beauty preparations.

## Stress and How to Cope With It

However well you plan your life and try to adapt to the changes it brings, there will be periods of stress. The most important thing is to recognize it for what it is and to learn to cope with it — something a younger person may not have the self control to manage adequately. The first thing to do is to identify the factors causing you stress. You'll have to look hard at your life, your personality and your reactions towards issues and other people. Perhaps it would be better to talk it over with another person, someone who is not too closely involved with you. Ask yourself if the circumstances cannot be altered so that less stress is caused. Perhaps someone near to you is suffering in some way and that is causing you stress as well — by helping, you both can achieve some peace of mind.

There are many organizations to help people with guidance and when you have no one else to talk to, they are a great help. Marriage guidance counsellors, priests, the vicar's wife, even a teacher at your child's school would be willing to listen if there is a problem at home. But in the long run it is you who must solve your own problems. One thing is certain — short term answers like drugs, such as tranquillizers and sleeping tablets, will not make the stressful problem go away. You are simply shelving it until you can no longer dodge the issue.

One of the most stressful parts of life is uncertainty — about the future, whether you will have a job in a few months time if the company is not doing well, whether your marriage will last if it has gone through a bad patch, whether a swelling you feel on your body will be malignant. The worst thing is to bottle feelings up and not do anything else about it. Think about what you can do positively to find out if the swelling is serious or not, what other job prospects there are, what you would do if you were left alone. Putting things off will only add to your stress.

Tensions, resentments and long bitter quarrels lead to stress and even to illness, mental or physical. Try to forgive others, which is not easy to do, but one of the greatest ways of relieving tension — just let things go! Try to forget the bad things that happened in the past and look hopefully to the future. After all, if you are feeling better due to exercise and a well-balanced diet, you are in good shape to face up to things positively. If you are in a time of stress, good food and exercise will not be doing you nearly so much good — all these things must be seen as a whole in your life.

Try to be self-critical. Listen to what others say to you, even if it is harsh — it may be justified. Think about it and act upon it if it is. Be more open with your closest friends and family — often misunderstandings arise when we are not careful enough to explain properly our motives and actions.

Above all take a few practical measures in your life. Don't work daily for hours on end — certainly no more than eight to ten hours. Give yourself time to eat and digest your balanced meal, eating slowly and chewing well. Practise meditation if you can, or listen for a while every day to some relaxing music, or carry out the relaxation exercises on page 72. Try to move at a steady pace — don't rush so much. Take at least ten minutes' exercise a day. Get plenty of sleep. Try to keep at least one day a week for other things apart from work, and at least one or two weeks a year for a holiday that gives you the chance to see different places and people. Make sure that you get enough fresh air — and sunshine when it is around. Work methodically through your set tasks, finishing one before you start another. Don't set unrealistic deadlines for yourself — and don't let others do so; instead, explain what you can achieve in the time given. Learn to leave what cannot be done in a day until the next one. When you tell someone that you cannot do a particular job in a given time, express yourself openly and without hostility. That goes for other discussions with people around you. Smile a lot more and you won't have that turned down mouth that is so ageing.

If work is causing you stress, see if anything realistic can be done about it, perhaps even retraining for something quite different. Many people who have been made redundant have begun a whole new way of life, starting a small business or shop, or even expanding a craft hobby into a viable money earner, which gives a great sense of achievement.

If you are unhappy over a relationship, take advice but don't rely on drugs for any sort of stress. The same goes for smoking and alcohol — they won't help in the long run, and will only ruin your health. Start a new absorbing hobby, go to an exercise class or take up yoga. Join a health club or leisure centre, take a regular massage. Concentrate on the present and the future and let the past go, with its memories, pleasant and unpleasant. Feel relaxed and happy and you'll feel fitter and younger, for far longer than you ever dreamed you could. Learn to be decisive — it's the indecision that will cause you more stress in the end. Be independent-minded and less reliant on others — another ageing sign. Learn to face the challenge and enjoy life even if it has been stressful in the past. Above all, think young, not old — be receptive to new ideas and the ideas of the younger people around you. Bridge that generation gap until, for you, it doesn't exist.

# Index

acid saturation, 9
acne, 56, 95
additives, in food, 24
aerobics, 83-86
Aerobics Institute, Dallas, 85
alcohol, 112-14
Almond Cleansing Cream, recipe for, 91
anaemia, 35, 42
Andes, the (S. America), 8, 13, 20, 21, 48
animal fats, 11, 22
astringents, 92
autogenics, 72

baldness, 36
bathing, 109-11
biotin, 36
Birkett, Dr Denis, 31
Bogomolets, Dr Alexander, 17
Bogomolets Institute, 17-18
brewer's yeast, 56-8
bronchitis, 115
*Bullworker*, the, 78

cabbage juice, 67
calcium, 41-2
cancer, 8, 14, 20, 34, 48, 49, 115
carbohydrates, 27-29
carotene, 34
Caucasus, the (USSR), 8, 13, 18, 19, 21
cholesterol, 24
citrus juices, 67-8
Cleanser, Light, recipe for, 91
cleansers, face, 90, 91
conditioners, hair, 106

constipation, 10, 31, 44
contraceptive pill, 35, 36, 45
Cooper, Dr Kenneth, 84
cosmetics, history of, 88-9
Crile, Dr George W., 9
Culpeper, Nicholas, 89

Davies, Dr David, 20
depression, 35
diabetes, 8, 55

eczema, 56
epilepsy, 36
exercise, importance of, 70
    machines, 78-80

facial exercises, 95
fats, 24-27
    polyunsaturated, 25
feet, care of, 99-101
fibre, in diet, 10, 30-3
folic acid, 36

gardening, organic, 120-22
Gerontology, Institute of, 19
goitre, 41, 43
Grant, Doris, 10
Grape Cure, the, 68

hair care, 103-108
hands, care of, 96-8
Hauser, Gayelord, 66, 70, 71, 99, 104, 114
Hay, Dr William Howard, 9, 14, 15

*Health Via Food*, 9, 15
heart disease, 8, 11, 20, 23, 26, 53, 85, 115
henna, 107
honey, 18-19, 62-5
Hunza, the (Pakistan), 8, 13-17, 21

infant mortality, 20
iodine, 41, 43
iron, 42-3
isometric exercises, 75-8

juices, raw, 65

Kordel, Lelord, 74

Lane, Dr William Arbuthnot, 18
longevity, 8

McCarrison, Dr Sir Robert, 13-17, 103
Madras, the, 13
magnesium, 41, 44
manicure, 97
Mayo Clinic, 70
menopause, 54
minerals, 39-41
moisturizers, 92, 93
monosodium glutamate, 47
muscles, voluntary, 75

nicotinic acid, 35

obesity, 24
oestrogens, 54
osteo-arthritis, 35
osteomalacia, 38, 42

pantothenic acid, 36
para-aminobenzoic acid (PABA), 36
pellagra, 35
phosphorus, 42
Pliny, 18
posture, good, 73
potassium, 44
Price, Dr Weston A., 103
propolis, 64
protein, 9, 29-30
pyorrhoea, 103
pyrodoxine, *see* vitamin $B_6$

refined foods, 8, 9, 23, 27, 28, 31, 41, 103
relaxation exercises, 71-3
rhubarb juice, 68
riboflavin, *see* vitamin $B_2$
royal jelly, 64

salt, *see* sodium chloride
Schultz, Dr J. H., 72
selenium, 48-9
shampoo, 105
Shute, Dr Wilfred, 56
skin creams, conditioning, 93
skin fresheners, 92
sleep, 111
smoking, 114-18
sodium chloride (salt), 46-8
stress, coping with, 122
sunbathing, 108
swimming, 80

teeth, care of, 101-103
texturized vegetable protein (tvp), 30
thiamin, *see* vitamin $B_1$

vegetables, to cook, 39
vitamins, 33-9
 A, 34, 45
 B complex, 34-6, 50
 $B_1$, 34
 $B_2$, 35
 $B_6$, 35
 $B_{12}$, 35
 C, 36
 D, 37-8, 41
 E, 38, 48, 53-6
 K, 38

water exercises, 80
wheatgerm, 41, 51-6
Wheatgerm Muffins, 52
wholefood diet, 10-11, 22, 32
Wholewheat Bread Rolls, 53
'wonder foods', 50

yoga, 71
yogurt, 58-62
 to make, 60-1

zinc, 41, 45